MODERN APPROACHES TO TEACHING POLITICAL SCIENCE

DR VIVEK SANJAY PAWAR

Made with ♥ on the Notion Press Platform
www.notionpress.com

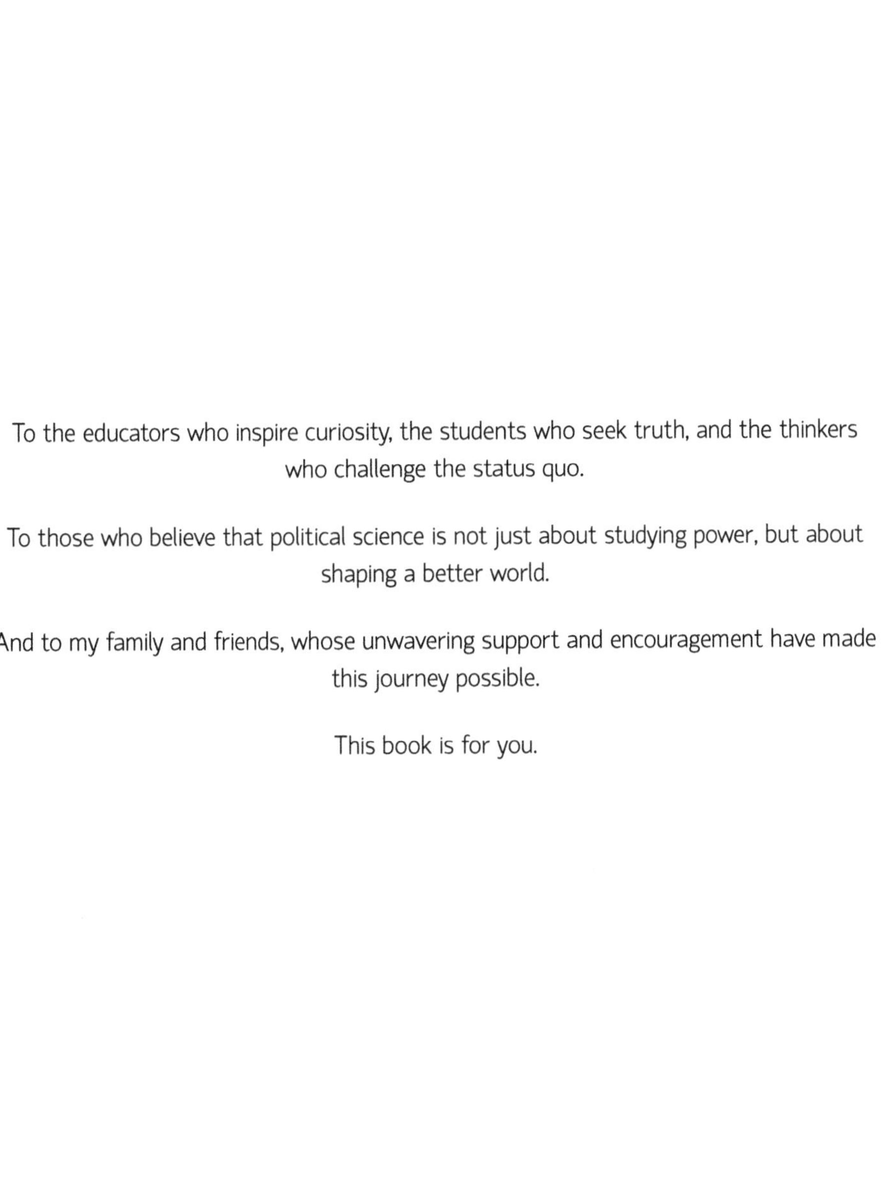

To the educators who inspire curiosity, the students who seek truth, and the thinkers who challenge the status quo.

To those who believe that political science is not just about studying power, but about shaping a better world.

And to my family and friends, whose unwavering support and encouragement have made this journey possible.

This book is for you.

Contents

Contents

Foreword

Political science is no longer confined to textbooks, lecture halls, and theoretical discussions. It has become an ever-evolving, dynamic field shaped by technology, data, and global interactions. The way we teach, learn, and engage with politics must adapt to this new reality. This book is a timely and necessary contribution to the modernization of political science education, providing a fresh perspective on how we can make the subject more engaging, relevant, and impactful.

In today's world, where artificial intelligence predicts election outcomes, social media influences governance, and digital tools transform policymaking, political science education must go beyond traditional teaching methods. The book you are about to read introduces innovative approaches such as flipped classrooms, Socratic seminars, political simulations, and AI-driven policy analysis. It challenges the status quo by integrating technology with political education and equipping students with the skills necessary for real-world applications.

What makes this book particularly valuable is its interdisciplinary approach. By blending insights from behavioural economics, psychology, data science, and media studies, it provides a holistic framework for understanding political processes. It encourages critical thinking, fosters analytical skills, and emphasizes ethical decision-making—qualities that are essential for future leaders, policymakers, and scholars.

As an educator, researcher, and political analyst, I believe that this book is an essential guide for anyone seeking to bridge the gap between traditional political science and the demands of a rapidly changing world. Whether you are an academic designing a future-ready curriculum, a student preparing for a career in politics or policy, or a professional looking to navigate the complexities of modern governance, this book will serve as an invaluable resource.

I commend the author for their vision and dedication to transforming political science education. The insights, case studies, and practical applications presented here will undoubtedly shape the way we think about politics in the years to come. It is my hope that this book inspires educators and students alike to embrace innovation, challenge conventional wisdom, and actively engage in the political realities

Preface

Political science is at a crossroads. The way we study, teach, and engage with politics is evolving at an unprecedented pace. In an era of rapid technological advancements, real-time political discourse on social media, and increasingly complex global challenges, traditional methods of political science education are no longer sufficient. This book is a response to that change—a guide to reimagining political science education for the 21st century.

As someone deeply invested in both academia and practical applications of political analysis, I have witnessed firsthand the shifting landscape of political education. The old ways of passive learning, rote memorization, and one-dimensional theoretical instruction are giving way to more interactive, data-driven, and interdisciplinary approaches. Today, political science students and educators must navigate a world where artificial intelligence predicts elections, digital media shapes public opinion, and behavioral insights influence policymaking. To stay relevant, we must embrace innovation while holding on to the core principles of critical thinking, democratic discourse, and ethical governance.

This book is designed for educators, students, researchers, and policymakers who seek to bridge the gap between traditional political science and modern methodologies. It explores how flipped classrooms, Socratic debates, simulations, and digital storytelling can revolutionize teaching. It delves into the role of AI, data analytics, and behavioral economics in understanding voter behavior and policymaking. It examines the challenges posed by misinformation, cyber warfare, and media manipulation, while also highlighting the opportunities presented by blockchain in governance and digital diplomacy.

The central aim of this book is to provide a roadmap for adapting political science education to contemporary needs. Whether you are an instructor looking for innovative teaching methods, a student eager to acquire skills for the modern job market, a researcher seeking new analytical tools, or a policymaker navigating the complexities of governance in a digital world, this book offers insights and strategies that will be of practical use.

Political science is not just an academic discipline—it is a field that shapes societies, influences decision-making, and drives change. By rethinking how we teach and learn it, we can better equip future generations to tackle the political challenges of tomorrow. My hope is that this book serves as both a resource and an inspiration for all those committed to making political science education more dynamic, relevant, and impactful.

• x •

Acknowledgements

Writing this book has been an enlightening journey, and it would not have been possible without the support, guidance, and inspiration of many individuals who have contributed in various ways.

First and foremost, I would like to express my deepest gratitude to the educators, researchers, and policymakers who are shaping the future of political science education. Their dedication to fostering critical thinking, interdisciplinary learning, and technological adaptation has been a guiding force throughout this work. The insights gained from countless discussions, academic papers, and real-world case studies have been invaluable in shaping the ideas presented here.

I am especially grateful to my mentors and colleagues who have provided invaluable feedback, encouragement, and intellectual support. Their perspectives have helped refine the core themes of this book, ensuring its relevance and impact for educators and students alike. Their unwavering belief in the importance of modernizing political science education has been a driving motivation behind this work.

To my students and fellow learners, I extend my heartfelt appreciation. Your curiosity, enthusiasm, and willingness to question conventional wisdom have been a source of constant inspiration. The classroom discussions, debates, and explorations into new methodologies have reinforced my belief that political science must evolve to meet the challenges of a rapidly changing world.

A special thanks to my friends and family for their patience and unwavering support during the writing process. Their encouragement, understanding, and belief in my vision have been instrumental in bringing this project to fruition. The long hours of research, writing, and revisions would not have been possible without their steadfast support.

Finally, I would like to acknowledge the contributions of the many scholars, thought leaders, and innovators whose work has paved the way for the ideas explored in this book. Their pioneering research in political science, technology, and education has provided the foundation upon which this book is built.

This book is dedicated to all those who believe in the transformative power of education and the need to continuously adapt to the evolving political landscape. It is my hope that the insights shared here will serve as a valuable resource for those committed to shaping the future of political science education.

Prologue

Politics is the force that shapes societies, defines leadership, and influences the course of history. Yet, the way we study political science has remained largely unchanged for decades, even as the world around us has transformed at an unprecedented pace. From the rise of social media-driven elections to artificial intelligence predicting voter behavior, the landscape of governance and political decision-making is no longer what it once was. This book is a response to that transformation—a call to rethink how we teach, learn, and engage with political science in the modern era.

The inspiration for this book comes from a growing realization that political education must evolve. Traditional methods, centered on theoretical discussions and static texts, are no longer sufficient in a world where real-time data, digital diplomacy, and behavioral psychology are reshaping governance. The students of today and the leaders of tomorrow need a dynamic, interdisciplinary, and technologically informed approach to political science—one that equips them not just with knowledge but with the skills to navigate the complexities of contemporary politics.

Throughout history, revolutions in political thought have often been driven by those who dared to ask new questions and challenge outdated norms. This book seeks to ignite that same spirit of innovation in political science education. By exploring modern teaching methods, data-driven decision-making, and the role of emerging technologies, it aims to provide a roadmap for the future of the discipline. Whether you are an educator seeking fresh teaching strategies, a student eager to apply political theory to real-world issues, or a policymaker navigating the digital age, this book offers insights that will help bridge the gap between tradition and modernity.

As you turn these pages, I invite you to embark on a journey that goes beyond textbooks and lectures—a journey into the future of political science. Let us embrace new ways of thinking, teaching, and understanding politics, ensuring that the next generation is not only well-informed but also well-prepared to shape the world they will inherit.

Introduction

CHAPTER ONE

Introduction

The Changing nature of Political Science Education

Political science education is undergoing a profound transformation, shaped by rapid technological advancements, evolving global dynamics, and shifting student expectations. Traditionally, political science was taught through lectures, textbooks, and theoretical discussions, with a strong emphasis on historical context and institutional analysis. While these methods remain valuable, they are no longer sufficient to prepare students for the complexities of modern governance, policy-making, and political analysis. Today's students are entering a world where politics is increasingly shaped by artificial intelligence, big data, social media, and digital diplomacy. As a result, educators must rethink how political science is taught, incorporating interdisciplinary approaches, interactive learning experiences, and real-world problem-solving.

The demand for practical skills, such as data analysis, policy writing, and digital literacy, has never been higher. Employers seek graduates who can navigate the fast-changing political landscape, analyze trends in real-time, and engage with the public through various media platforms. Meanwhile, students are looking for more than just theoretical knowledge—they want hands-on experiences, opportunities for debate, and exposure to global perspectives. The rise of online learning platforms, AI-driven education tools, and immersive simulations presents an opportunity to bridge the gap between academic knowledge and practical application. From flipped classrooms and Socratic seminars to role-playing exercises and data-driven political analysis, new teaching methods are revolutionizing how political science is learned and applied.

In this changing landscape, educators must also address the ethical and societal implications of technological advancements in politics. Misinformation, cyber warfare, and AI-driven propaganda challenge democratic institutions, making it crucial for students to develop critical thinking and media literacy skills. At the same time, the integration of behavioral economics, psychology, and data science into political studies opens up new possibilities for understanding voter behavior and shaping public policy.

This book explores how political science education must adapt to remain relevant in the 21st century. By examining innovative teaching strategies, emerging technologies, and real-world case studies, it provides educators and students with the tools needed to thrive in an increasingly complex political environment. The goal is not just to modernize political science education but to empower the next generation of leaders, analysts, and policymakers with the skills they need to shape the future of democracy.

Why traditional political science teaching methods are evolving

Traditional political science teaching methods are evolving because the world of politics itself has transformed dramatically. In the past, political science education was largely theoretical, relying on lectures, textbooks, and historical case studies to explain government structures, ideologies, and policy-making processes. While these methods provided a strong foundation, they often failed to equip students with the practical skills needed to navigate the complexities of modern governance. Today, politics is no longer confined to parliaments, courts, and academic discussions; it unfolds in real-time on social media, in data analytics models, and through artificial intelligence-driven campaigns. This shift demands a new approach to teaching—one that is more interactive, interdisciplinary, and technologically advanced.

One of the primary reasons for this evolution is the changing expectations of students and employers. Political science graduates are no longer limited to careers in academia, government, or law; they now find opportunities in political consulting, digital campaigning, data analysis, journalism, and even entrepreneurship. As a result, universities must move beyond rote memorization of political theories and instead focus on equipping students with analytical, research, and communication skills that align with contemporary job markets. Additionally, the rapid rise of misinformation, digital propaganda, and cyber warfare has made it essential for political science education to emphasize critical thinking and media literacy. Without these skills, students may struggle to differentiate between credible information and manipulative narratives in today's highly polarized political climate.

Technology has also played a crucial role in driving this change. With the availability of massive datasets on voter behavior, public opinion, and international conflicts, political science has increasingly embraced data-driven methodologies. Traditional approaches that relied on qualitative analysis alone are being complemented—or even replaced—by quantitative techniques such as predictive modeling, machine learning, and GIS mapping. This shift requires educators to introduce students to programming languages like Python and R, as well as tools for real-time political analysis.

Moreover, the very nature of political engagement has changed. In the past, political debates took place in legislative chambers or through traditional media, but now, social media platforms like Twitter, YouTube, and TikTok shape public discourse. Understanding digital activism, online diplomacy, and the role of AI in shaping political narratives has become as important as studying classical political theories. Universities must therefore integrate these modern developments into their curricula, using tools such as flipped classrooms, Model UN simulations, and AI-driven policy games to enhance student engagement.

Ultimately, political science education must evolve to remain relevant in a world where politics is fast-paced, data-driven, and digitally interconnected. By embracing innovative teaching methods, interdisciplinary approaches, and real-world applications, educators can ensure that students are not just passive learners but active participants in shaping the future of governance and democracy.

The need for critical thinking, interdisciplinary knowledge, and technological adaptation

In today's rapidly changing political landscape, the need for critical thinking, interdisciplinary knowledge, and technological adaptation in political science education has never been more urgent. The traditional approach to teaching politics—relying heavily on historical case studies, static theories, and institutional analysis—fails to equip students with the skills necessary to navigate modern governance, policymaking, and global affairs. The increasing complexity of political challenges, from misinformation to cyber warfare, requires a new educational model that fosters analytical thinking, cross-disciplinary learning, and technological proficiency.

Critical thinking is at the heart of political science, yet it is often undermined by outdated teaching methods that focus on memorization rather than analysis. Today's students are exposed to an overwhelming amount of political content through social media, news outlets, and academic sources, making it essential for them to differentiate between credible information and propaganda. Without strong critical thinking skills, they may fall prey to misinformation, manipulation, or ideological bias. To counter this, political science education must prioritize debate, discussion, and case-based learning. Methods such as Socratic seminars, structured debates, and role-playing simulations push students to question assumptions, analyze opposing viewpoints, and develop well-reasoned arguments. These approaches not only enhance their ability to think independently but also prepare them for real-world decision-making in political analysis, policy formulation, and governance.

Interdisciplinary knowledge is another crucial aspect of modern political science education. Politics does not exist in isolation—it intersects with economics, sociology, psychology, data science, law, and environmental studies. Understanding voter behavior, for example, requires insights from psychology and behavioral economics, while analyzing international relations demands knowledge of history, cultural studies, and global trade. The rise of data-driven decision-making means that students must also engage with statistics, artificial intelligence, and computational social science. By integrating these diverse fields, educators can offer a more holistic understanding of political systems and equip students with the ability to apply their knowledge in various domains, from diplomacy to corporate governance.

Technological adaptation is perhaps the most pressing need in political science education. The digital revolution has transformed the way politics operates, from AI-powered election campaigns to real-time public opinion analysis. Traditional teaching methods that ignore these advancements leave students unprepared for the realities of modern governance. Political science programs must therefore incorporate digital tools such as data analytics software, GIS mapping for geopolitical analysis, and AI-driven simulations of policymaking and crisis management. Additionally, emerging platforms like MOOCs (Massive Open Online Courses) and AI-powered learning assistants provide new ways to personalize education and enhance engagement.

To remain relevant, political science education must evolve to include critical thinking, interdisciplinary approaches, and technological proficiency. A curriculum that embraces these elements will not only produce informed citizens but also skilled professionals who can shape public policy, analyze global trends, and lead in an era of rapid political and technological change. By fostering adaptability, intellectual curiosity, and digital literacy, educators can prepare students to navigate the complexities of 21st-century politics with confidence and competence.

Audience: Educators, students, researchers, policymakers

Political science education is no longer just about understanding government structures or memorizing political theories—it is about equipping individuals with the tools to analyze, predict, and engage with an ever-changing global landscape. Whether you are an educator shaping the next generation of political thinkers, a student preparing for a career in policy or governance, a researcher delving into the complexities of political behavior, or a policymaker making crucial decisions that affect millions, the ability to think critically, integrate interdisciplinary knowledge, and adapt to technological advancements is now a necessity.

For educators, the challenge lies in transforming traditional political science instruction into an interactive, skills-based learning experience. Lectures alone no longer suffice in an age where politics unfolds in real-time on digital platforms. To keep students engaged and prepare them for the future, educators must incorporate experiential learning methods such as flipped classrooms, structured debates, policy simulations, and AI-driven political analysis tools. The shift from passive learning to active participation fosters deeper understanding and analytical skills, making students more effective thinkers and problem solvers.

Students, on the other hand, must recognize that their political science education is not just about passing exams but about developing a versatile skill set that applies across various industries. Careers in diplomacy, journalism, governance, public policy, data analytics, and even entrepreneurship require an understanding of political structures combined with expertise in data interpretation, digital media analysis, and behavioral science. The ability to synthesize information, conduct research, and communicate ideas persuasively will determine success in a world where misinformation and political polarization are rampant.

For researchers, the evolution of political science offers new methodologies and tools to analyze political phenomena with greater precision. Traditional qualitative approaches remain important, but the integration of data science, machine learning, and AI-driven analytics has expanded the scope of political research. Predicting election outcomes, understanding voter behavior, and assessing the impact of policy decisions now require interdisciplinary collaboration, bringing together political science with psychology, economics, and computer science. The challenge for researchers is to balance theoretical insights with empirical data to produce meaningful, policy-relevant findings.

Policymakers must also adapt to these changes by leveraging new technologies to make informed decisions. With real-time access to public opinion trends, policy impact assessments, and crisis simulations, modern governance demands a data-driven approach. Effective policymaking is no longer just about political ideology—it requires understanding complex systems, anticipating public reactions, and implementing solutions based on empirical evidence. Moreover, policymakers must be equipped to counter digital threats such as cyber warfare, deepfake propaganda, and AI-driven disinformation campaigns that can destabilize democratic institutions.

In this rapidly evolving landscape, political science education must bridge the gap between theory and practice. By fostering critical thinking, interdisciplinary learning, and technological adaptation, we can prepare the next generation of political leaders, analysts, and decision-makers to navigate the complexities of governance in the 21st century. Whether you are an educator, student, researcher, or policymaker, the future of political science is in your hands—how you engage with it will shape the policies, institutions, and societies of tomorrow.

Innovative Pedagogical Strategies in Political Science

Beyond Lectures – Engaging Political Science Students

Active Learning vs. Passive Learning

For years, classrooms have followed a predictable pattern: the teacher stands at the front, delivering a lecture while students sit quietly, taking notes. This method, known as passive learning, has long been the backbone of education, particularly in subjects like political science. But here's the problem—politics isn't just about memorizing dates, theories, and policies. It's about debate, discussion, and real-world application. If we want students to truly understand how governments function, why policies succeed or fail, or how ideologies shape the world, we need to move beyond rote memorization. That's where active learning comes in.

Passive learning has its place—it provides structure and ensures students cover a broad syllabus. But it also has major flaws. Think about it: how much do you really remember from a class where you just sat and listened? Probably not much. That's because passive learning is just that—passive. It doesn't engage students, doesn't challenge them to think critically, and doesn't encourage them to apply what they learn. Political science, in particular, demands more. It's a subject that thrives on debate, questioning, and critical analysis. Simply reading about democracy in a textbook won't teach students why it matters, how it can be threatened, or how it adapts over time.

Now, imagine a different classroom. Instead of a one-way lecture, students are engaged in a heated debate about the effectiveness of socialism versus capitalism. They're not just learning about these ideologies; they're defending them, challenging opposing viewpoints, and figuring out real-world applications. This is active learning in action. By participating in discussions, simulations, and role-playing exercises, students absorb knowledge in a way that sticks. They aren't just memorizing facts; they're applying them.

One of the most effective ways to make political science come alive is through case studies. Instead of just reading about revolutions, students analyze real-world events—the Arab Spring, Brexit, the fall of the Berlin Wall. They break down the causes, the political responses, and the long-term impact. This makes learning feel less like an abstract theory and more like a detective story, where they're piecing together clues to understand how history shapes the present.

Debates and role-playing exercises are another powerful tool. Imagine students taking on the roles of different world leaders during a climate change summit. One group represents a developing nation pushing for financial aid to combat environmental damage, while another defends the interests of a wealthy industrialized country reluctant to cut emissions. Suddenly, political theory isn't just something they study—it's something they experience. They learn negotiation skills, understand different perspectives, and realize the complexities of governance.

Then there are simulations—digital tools that let students step into the shoes of policymakers, diplomats, or activists. Imagine an AI-driven scenario where students must manage an economic crisis, negotiate a peace treaty, or craft a political campaign. These experiences provide hands-on learning that no textbook can match. They prepare students for real-world challenges, showing them the impact of political decisions in a controlled, interactive environment.

The Socratic method, another active learning technique, encourages students to question everything. Instead of just accepting a political theory at face value, they engage in structured discussions, exploring its strengths and weaknesses. This builds not just knowledge, but also the ability to think critically—an essential skill in today's complex political landscape.

Beyond the classroom, active learning can extend into real political engagement. Students who participate in community projects, advocacy groups, or even local governance initiatives see firsthand how policies affect people's lives. They aren't just learning about political science—they're living it.

Of course, shifting from passive to active learning isn't easy. Many educators are accustomed to traditional lecture-based teaching. It takes more time and effort to plan debates, design simulations, and facilitate discussions. And in large classrooms, ensuring that every student participates can be a challenge. But the benefits far outweigh the difficulties. A student who debates, questions, and applies political concepts will always have a deeper understanding than one who simply memorizes information for a test.

The world of politics is constantly evolving, and education needs to evolve with it. We can no longer afford to teach political science as a collection of static facts. It must be dynamic, engaging, and relevant. By embracing active learning, we can create classrooms that don't just teach political theory but shape the next generation of thinkers, leaders, and change-makers. After all, politics isn't just something to study—it's something to participate in. And that's a lesson best learned by doing.

Flipped Classrooms: How pre-class reading & in-class discussions work

Education has traditionally followed a straightforward approach: students attend lectures, take notes, and then go home to complete assignments. This system has been in place for generations, but it has its drawbacks. Many students struggle to grasp new concepts during lectures, often feeling overwhelmed or unable to keep up with the pace of teaching. By the time they attempt their homework, they may lack the foundational understanding needed to complete it effectively. This is where the flipped classroom model comes in—a revolutionary shift that turns traditional learning on its head.

In a flipped classroom, students engage with new material before they even step into the classroom. Instead of first encountering a concept through a lecture, they are assigned pre-class readings, video lectures, or interactive modules. This allows them to learn at their own pace, pausing, rewinding, or re-reading as necessary. The classroom then becomes a space for deeper discussion, problem-solving, and collaborative activities rather than passive listening. This model shifts the teacher's role from being a lecturer to a facilitator, guiding students as they actively engage with the material.

Pre-class reading is a crucial component of the flipped classroom. By assigning relevant materials—textbook chapters, articles, or even recorded video lectures—students arrive in class with a basic understanding of the topic. This preparation ensures that valuable class time is not spent simply introducing concepts but rather exploring their applications and implications. It also encourages students to take responsibility for their learning, developing independent study habits that are essential for success in higher education and professional life.

However, simply expecting students to read or watch material before class isn't enough. The key to making a flipped classroom effective lies in how that preparation is reinforced during in-class sessions. Discussions become the heart of the learning experience. Instead of passively receiving information, students engage in debates, ask questions, and clarify doubts. They interact with their peers, hear diverse perspectives, and deepen their understanding through active participation. This method also encourages critical thinking—students don't just learn facts, they learn to analyze and apply them.

One of the greatest advantages of this approach is that it allows for more personalized learning. In a traditional classroom, students with different learning speeds often struggle—some feel left behind, while others feel unchallenged. In a flipped classroom, students can review pre-class materials as many times as needed, ensuring they grasp the basics before class. Then, during discussions, the teacher can focus on addressing specific areas where students need more clarity, rather than delivering a one-size-fits-all lecture.

Additionally, this method fosters a more engaging and interactive classroom environment. Instead of passively listening to a lecture, students engage in group activities, case studies, and problem-solving exercises. They apply what they've learned in real-time, reinforcing their understanding through practice. The classroom transforms into a collaborative space where learning is active rather than passive.

Despite its many benefits, the flipped classroom model does come with challenges. Not all students may have access to the necessary resources outside of class, such as stable internet connections or quiet study spaces. Additionally, some students may not complete the pre-class work, which can limit their ability to participate effectively in discussions. To address this, teachers can provide multiple formats of learning materials—such as printable summaries for those who prefer reading and videos for visual learners. Regular check-ins or quick quizzes can also encourage students to complete their pre-class preparation.

Moreover, educators must be prepared for a shift in their teaching style. Transitioning from a traditional lecture-based approach to a flipped classroom requires careful planning. Teachers need to create engaging pre-class materials, design meaningful in-class activities, and facilitate discussions effectively. This demands more initial effort but ultimately leads to a more rewarding and effective learning experience for students.

The flipped classroom model is more than just a trend—it's a powerful way to make education more student-centered, interactive, and effective. By allowing students to learn at their own pace before class and then actively engage with the material during discussions, this approach bridges the gap between theory and application. It not only improves retention and understanding but also prepares students for real-world challenges, where critical thinking and collaboration are key. In a world where information is readily available, the ability to analyze, discuss, and apply knowledge is more important than ever—and that's exactly what a flipped classroom fosters.

Socratic Seminars & Structured Debates

Education is most effective when it encourages students to think, question, and engage in meaningful dialogue. Too often, traditional classrooms rely on passive learning methods, where students listen to lectures and memorize information without truly analyzing or challenging ideas. This is where Socratic seminars and structured debates play a transformative role. These approaches not only deepen students' understanding of complex topics but also cultivate essential skills like critical thinking, communication, and reasoning.

A Socratic seminar is based on the teaching style of the ancient Greek philosopher Socrates, who believed that questioning was the key to deep learning. Instead of providing direct answers, Socratic seminars encourage students to explore topics through thoughtful, open-ended discussions. The teacher acts as a facilitator, guiding students through a series of questions that help them uncover deeper meanings and connections. The goal is not simply to reach a correct answer but to engage in a process of intellectual discovery.

In a Socratic seminar, students are presented with a text, concept, or problem in advance. They read and analyze the material before coming to class, preparing questions and insights. When the discussion begins, the teacher poses an initial question—one that is broad and thought-provoking, designed to spark debate rather than elicit a simple response. For example, in a political science class, students might be asked: Is democracy always the best form of government? This question has no single correct answer but instead invites students to examine historical examples, ethical considerations, and political theories.

As students engage in dialogue, they are encouraged to listen actively, build on one another's ideas, and ask their own questions. The discussion flows naturally, with students critically evaluating arguments and refining their viewpoints. Unlike traditional classroom discussions where a teacher dominates the conversation, Socratic seminars create a student-driven learning experience. This process not only deepens comprehension but also helps students develop confidence in expressing their ideas.

While Socratic seminars emphasize open-ended discussion, structured debates take a more formal approach, requiring students to construct clear arguments and defend their positions. Debates provide an opportunity for students to practice persuasive speaking, logical reasoning, and evidence-based argumentation. They also introduce students to the reality that political and social issues are rarely black-and-white—most topics have multiple perspectives, each with valid points.

In a structured debate, students are divided into teams, each assigned a specific position on an issue. They must research their stance thoroughly, gathering evidence and anticipating counterarguments. The debate follows a set format, typically including opening statements, rebuttals, cross-examinations, and closing arguments. The structure ensures that every participant has a chance to speak and that arguments are well-organized.

For instance, a debate on government surveillance versus individual privacy might have one team arguing that surveillance is necessary for national security, while the opposing team defends personal freedoms. As students present their cases, they must not only articulate their own points clearly but also respond to challenges from the opposing side. This back-and-forth exchange hones their ability to think quickly, counter objections, and refine their arguments under pressure.

One of the most valuable aspects of structured debates is that they teach students to see both sides of an issue. Even if they personally disagree with the position they are assigned, they must research and argue for it convincingly. This builds empathy and a deeper understanding of opposing viewpoints—a crucial skill in today's polarized world.

Both Socratic seminars and structured debates contribute to a richer, more interactive learning experience. Instead of passively absorbing information, students engage with ideas actively, questioning assumptions and defending their perspectives. These methods also cultivate essential life skills: the ability to communicate effectively, think critically, and engage in respectful discourse.

However, implementing these approaches requires preparation and guidance. Teachers must ensure that discussions remain respectful and constructive, providing clear expectations for participation. It's also important to create an inclusive environment where every student feels encouraged to contribute, regardless of their confidence level.

Ultimately, Socratic seminars and structured debates transform the classroom into a dynamic space where students don't just learn facts—they learn how to think. They move beyond memorization and develop the intellectual skills necessary to navigate complex issues, both in academia and in real life. By fostering curiosity, dialogue, and critical reasoning, these methods prepare students not only to understand the world but also to engage with it thoughtfully and effectively.

Role-Playing & Simulations: UN simulations, elections, crisis decision-making

Learning is most impactful when students are placed in real-world scenarios where they must think critically, communicate effectively, and make decisions under pressure. Role-playing and simulations bring education to life by immersing students in practical experiences that mirror real-world challenges. Whether it is a United Nations simulation, a mock election, or a crisis decision-making exercise, these interactive methods provide students with invaluable insights into global affairs, governance, and strategic thinking. Unlike traditional lecture-based learning, where students passively absorb information, role-playing and simulations require active engagement, fostering a deeper understanding of complex issues and improving essential skills like negotiation, problem-solving, and leadership.

A United Nations simulation, often referred to as Model United Nations (MUN), allows students to take on the roles of diplomats representing different countries. Participants engage in formal debates, draft resolutions, and negotiate solutions to pressing global issues such as climate change, international conflicts, and human rights violations. This form of experiential learning compels students to research their assigned nation's policies, historical positions, and geopolitical strategies, preparing them for intense discussions. As the simulation unfolds, students must navigate alliances, respond to diplomatic challenges, and refine their public speaking abilities. By stepping into the shoes of policymakers, students gain firsthand experience of how international diplomacy functions, learning that global politics is a delicate balance of negotiation, persuasion, and compromise. Through this process, they also develop a deeper appreciation for diverse perspectives and the complexities of decision-making on a global stage.

Mock elections provide another powerful simulation where students experience the electoral process firsthand, from campaigning to voting and policy formulation. Instead of studying democracy as a distant concept, students actively participate by forming political parties, developing policy platforms, and engaging in debates. They learn how political messaging shapes public opinion, how electoral systems influence outcomes, and why voter participation is crucial in a democracy. Candidates must craft persuasive speeches, address pressing social issues, and respond to challenging questions from their peers. Campaign strategies such as advertising, public rallies, and media interactions bring the simulation to life, showing students the intricacies of running for office. The election process itself—complete with voter registration, ballot casting, and vote counting—reinforces the significance of fair elections and democratic responsibility. This simulation fosters civic engagement and encourages students to become informed voters, making them more aware of the impact of governance on their everyday lives.

Crisis decision-making exercises take simulations to an even more intense level, requiring students to respond to high-stakes scenarios where rapid thinking and teamwork are essential. In a national security crisis, students may assume roles as government officials tasked with handling an international conflict, weighing intelligence reports, and deciding on diplomatic or military strategies. They must anticipate potential threats, engage in negotiations with other nations, and justify their decisions in front of a critical audience. Similarly, an economic crisis simulation could have students managing a financial downturn, forcing them to make tough choices about interest rates, trade policies, and fiscal stimulus measures. These exercises expose students to the reality that leaders must often make decisions with incomplete information, balancing short-term risks with long-term consequences. Another example is a pandemic response simulation, where students take on the roles of health ministers, scientists, and government leaders working together to contain a public health emergency. They must allocate medical resources, design public health campaigns, and respond to misinformation, all while considering economic and social impacts. Such simulations prepare students for the complexities of crisis leadership and reinforce the importance of adaptability, data-driven decision-making, and ethical responsibility.

The effectiveness of role-playing and simulations lies in their ability to make learning experiential and deeply personal. When students are actively involved in solving problems, rather than just reading about them, they retain knowledge more effectively and develop skills that are applicable beyond the classroom. These exercises encourage students to see issues from multiple perspectives, helping them build empathy and a broader worldview. The dynamic nature of these simulations also makes them more engaging, turning abstract theories into tangible experiences. Students are not just learning about international relations, governance, or crisis management; they are living through the challenges, frustrations, and triumphs of those roles.

Beyond academic benefits, role-playing and simulations cultivate essential life skills such as teamwork, communication, and adaptability. Public speaking confidence improves as students present their ideas and defend their positions in high-pressure situations. Critical thinking is sharpened as they assess risks, challenge assumptions, and make real-time decisions. Leadership abilities grow as students learn to inspire, negotiate, and navigate group dynamics. These skills are not just valuable for students interested in political science or diplomacy but are crucial for any profession that requires strategic thinking and decision-making.

The true power of these simulations is that they provide students with a sense of agency and responsibility. They move beyond passive learning and become active participants in shaping outcomes, whether they are drafting a resolution in a UN committee, persuading voters in an election, or managing a crisis under tight deadlines. This empowerment creates a lasting impact, making students more engaged citizens and better problem-solvers in the real world. As education continues to evolve, integrating simulations and role-playing into the curriculum will be key in preparing students not just to understand the world but to engage with it meaningfully and lead with confidence.

CHAPTER THREE

Gamification and Experiential Learning in Political Science

Model UN, Model Parliament & Mock Court Trials

Experiential learning is at its most effective when students are given the opportunity to step into real-world roles and engage with complex issues firsthand. Model United Nations (Model UN), Model Parliament, and Mock Court Trials are three of the most dynamic and impactful simulations that prepare students for leadership, policy-making, and legal reasoning. Each of these exercises immerses students in decision-making scenarios, challenging them to think critically, collaborate effectively, and articulate their perspectives persuasively. These simulations not only deepen students' understanding of international relations, governance, and the judiciary but also develop their research skills, public speaking confidence, and problem-solving abilities.

Model United Nations is one of the most widely recognized academic simulations, allowing students to role-play as diplomats representing different countries. In this setting, participants debate pressing global issues, draft resolutions, and engage in diplomatic negotiations. Each student is assigned a country and must research its foreign policy, historical positions, and alliances. The debates follow formal parliamentary procedures, with students delivering speeches, making motions, and responding to real-time developments. The simulation covers a range of topics, including climate change, human rights, disarmament, and global security. As delegates, students must navigate international conflicts, form coalitions, and seek compromises that reflect their assigned country's interests while working toward global solutions. The experience teaches students about the complexities of diplomacy, the importance of soft power, and the delicate balance of national interests and international cooperation. It also fosters an appreciation for diverse viewpoints, encouraging students to engage in respectful dialogue and thoughtful negotiation.

Model Parliament takes students into the heart of the legislative process, simulating the functioning of a national or state parliament. Participants take on roles such as Members of Parliament (MPs), ministers, opposition leaders, and the Speaker of the House. The simulation begins with the introduction of bills, followed by debates, question hours, and voting on policies. Through this process, students learn about law-making, political ideologies, and the challenges of governance. They engage in passionate discussions on economic policies, social justice, and national security, often mirroring real-world political debates. The experience also highlights the importance of checks and balances, the role of the opposition in democracy, and the intricacies of parliamentary procedures. Model Parliament encourages students to critically analyze policy decisions, develop persuasive arguments, and engage in evidence-based discussions. Beyond academic knowledge, it cultivates leadership skills, teamwork, and an understanding of the responsibilities that come with public service. Students also gain insight into how political discourse shapes the laws that govern society and how democratic processes function in practice.

Mock Court Trials provide students with an in-depth understanding of the legal system by simulating real courtroom proceedings. In this setting, students assume the roles of judges, lawyers, plaintiffs, defendants, and witnesses. The trials are based on real or fictional legal cases, covering issues such as constitutional rights, criminal justice, and civil disputes. Each participant must prepare their arguments, examine evidence, and cross-examine witnesses to build a compelling case. The simulation follows courtroom procedures, including opening statements, witness testimonies, objections, and closing arguments. The experience teaches students the fundamentals of legal reasoning, judicial ethics, and the importance of due process. It also develops critical thinking skills as students must analyze legal principles, construct logical arguments, and anticipate counterarguments from the opposing side. Public speaking and persuasive communication are put to the test, as students must defend their positions before a judge or jury. For those interested in law, Mock Court Trials provide a valuable preview of legal careers, but even for those pursuing other fields, the exercise enhances logical reasoning, argumentation skills, and the ability to present ideas convincingly.

Each of these simulations—Model UN, Model Parliament, and Mock Court Trials—immerses students in the realities of governance, diplomacy, and law. They move beyond theoretical learning and offer a hands-on experience that fosters a deeper appreciation for the institutions that shape societies. The skills developed through these exercises, including research, debate, negotiation, and problem-solving, are universally applicable and prepare students for a wide range of careers. Moreover, these activities cultivate a sense of civic responsibility, encouraging students to become informed and engaged citizens.

What makes these simulations particularly powerful is their ability to instill confidence in students. Whether they are standing at the podium in a Model UN assembly, defending a legal argument in a courtroom, or debating policies in a parliamentary session, they learn to express their thoughts with clarity and conviction. They also gain an appreciation for the complexities of decision-making, realizing that real-world leaders must weigh multiple perspectives, anticipate consequences, and find balanced solutions. The structured yet dynamic nature of these activities ensures that learning is both rigorous and enjoyable.

Beyond the academic benefits, participation in these simulations often sparks lifelong interests in international relations, politics, and law. Many students who engage in Model UN go on to pursue careers in diplomacy or international organizations. Those who excel in Model Parliament may be inspired to enter public service or political leadership. Mock Court Trials often ignite a passion for justice and legal advocacy. These simulations serve as a gateway to real-world impact, empowering students to think critically about the world around them and take proactive steps toward positive change.

As education continues to evolve, incorporating experiential learning methods like these will be essential in preparing students not just to understand governance, diplomacy, and law, but to actively participate in shaping the future. By engaging in these structured yet dynamic exercises, students develop the skills, confidence, and mindset needed to navigate complex challenges and become thoughtful, informed, and responsible global citizens.

Political Science Escape Rooms: Problem-solving via historical & policy dilemmas

Escape rooms have become a popular and engaging way to encourage problem-solving, teamwork, and critical thinking. When applied to political science education, they transform historical and policy dilemmas into interactive challenges that require students to analyze complex situations, decode information, and work collaboratively to reach a solution. Political science escape rooms are designed to immerse students in realistic scenarios, where they must apply their knowledge of governance, diplomacy, and policy-making to "escape" from a simulated crisis or historical event. This gamified approach not only makes learning more dynamic and enjoyable but also deepens students' understanding of political processes, decision-making under pressure, and the consequences of historical and policy choices.

One of the most compelling aspects of political science escape rooms is their ability to recreate historical turning points. For example, students may be placed in the middle of the Cuban Missile Crisis, tasked with navigating diplomatic negotiations to prevent nuclear war. To "escape," they must analyze intelligence reports, interpret classified documents, and make strategic decisions based on the policies of the U.S., Soviet Union, and Cuba. Similarly, an escape room could center around drafting the U.S. Constitution, where students must compromise between competing political factions to finalize key provisions before the deadline. These experiences provide a hands-on approach to history, allowing students to engage with primary sources, debate ethical dilemmas, and develop a deeper appreciation for the complexities of political decision-making.

Policy-oriented escape rooms, on the other hand, place students in contemporary governance challenges. Imagine a scenario where students take on the roles of policymakers in a government cabinet, facing a climate change emergency. To succeed, they must analyze data, negotiate with various interest groups, and formulate an action plan that satisfies both economic and environmental concerns. Another escape room might simulate a refugee crisis, requiring participants to balance humanitarian aid, national security, and international law. These exercises force students to confront the realities of policy-making, understanding that decisions are rarely black and white. They must weigh competing interests, anticipate unintended consequences, and find solutions that align with legal and ethical considerations.

The design of these escape rooms often includes puzzles that reflect real-world political challenges. For instance, students might decipher coded messages to uncover a diplomatic plot, match legal precedents to their corresponding court rulings to advance a civil rights case, or piece together a historical timeline to prevent the outbreak of war. Clues could be hidden within speeches, treaties, or campaign posters, requiring students to apply their knowledge of political history and theory to progress through the game. These activities enhance analytical thinking, research skills, and the ability to synthesize complex information—a crucial skill set for students of political science.

What makes political science escape rooms particularly effective is their emphasis on teamwork and communication. Unlike traditional assessments, where students work individually, these simulations require them to collaborate, delegate tasks, and strategize under time constraints. Each team member brings different strengths—some may excel at historical analysis, others at logical reasoning, and others at persuasive argumentation. This mirrors real-world political environments, where successful governance depends on cooperation among diverse stakeholders. The sense of urgency created by the escape room format also enhances engagement, keeping students actively involved in problem-solving rather than passively absorbing information.

Beyond the classroom, these experiences prepare students for careers in politics, law, international relations, and public administration. They cultivate skills that are essential for these fields, such as crisis management, negotiation, ethical reasoning, and decision-making under pressure. More importantly, they encourage students to think critically about governance and public policy, equipping them with the mindset needed to tackle real-world challenges.

As education evolves, incorporating gamification and interactive learning methods like escape rooms can revolutionize the way political science is taught. By turning abstract theories and historical events into tangible, immersive experiences, political science escape rooms make learning more engaging, impactful, and memorable. They ensure that students are not just passive learners of history and policy but active participants in understanding and shaping the political landscape.

AI-driven political games for policy decision-making and elections

AI-driven political games are transforming the way students and professionals engage with policy decision-making and electoral processes. These simulations use artificial intelligence to create dynamic, evolving scenarios where players must navigate real-world political challenges, make strategic decisions, and respond to unpredictable events. Unlike traditional methods of studying governance and elections, AI-driven games provide an interactive, immersive experience that enhances critical thinking, problem-solving, and an understanding of political systems. By leveraging machine learning, big data, and real-time simulations, these games allow users to explore the complexities of governance, international relations, and electoral strategies in ways that traditional classroom learning cannot replicate.

One of the most exciting applications of AI in political gaming is policy decision-making simulations. In these games, players take on the roles of government officials, presidents, prime ministers, or legislators, tasked with managing a country's affairs. The AI generates realistic economic, social, and geopolitical challenges based on historical data and current global trends. For example, a player acting as the President of a nation may need to respond to an economic recession, balance a budget, negotiate trade agreements, or handle an international conflict. The AI continuously adapts to the player's choices, leading to complex cause-and-effect chains that mirror real-life governance. If a leader imposes high taxes, the AI may simulate citizen unrest, business opposition, or political backlash. If a leader invests in renewable energy, the game may generate climate improvements but also economic resistance from traditional industries. This dynamic response system ensures that no two gameplay experiences are the same, making learning more engaging and thought-provoking.

Another crucial area where AI-driven political games are making an impact is in election strategy and campaign management. In these simulations, players step into the shoes of a political candidate or campaign manager, strategizing how to win elections at various levels—local, national, or international. The AI-driven system incorporates voter behavior analytics, demographic trends, media influence, and real-time polling data, simulating the complexities of a modern election. Players must craft speeches, manage campaign funds, target key voter groups, respond to media scandals, and engage in debates. The AI continuously updates voter sentiment based on the player's decisions, making elections highly competitive and realistic. These games allow students to experiment with different campaign strategies, from grassroots mobilization to digital advertising, and observe the consequences of their choices in real-time. By simulating the unpredictability of elections—such as last-minute controversies, shifting public opinion, or external crises—these games prepare users for the fast-paced and high-stakes nature of political campaigning.

AI also enhances international relations and diplomacy simulations by creating realistic diplomatic scenarios where players act as global leaders, foreign ministers, or UN representatives. In these simulations, AI models global political behavior by tracking military conflicts, trade negotiations, and alliances. Players must engage in diplomacy, sign treaties, impose sanctions, or broker peace agreements, all while considering the interests of various nations. The AI reacts to every move, forcing players to anticipate consequences and adapt to shifting geopolitical landscapes. This type of simulation teaches students about international law, the art of negotiation, and the role of power dynamics in diplomacy.

Beyond academic settings, AI-driven political games are also being used in policy research and professional training. Governments, think tanks, and political strategists use these simulations to test policy initiatives before implementation. By running AI-generated scenarios, policymakers can analyze potential outcomes of policy decisions, predict public reactions, and refine strategies before taking real-world actions. For example, an AI-driven game could simulate the introduction of universal basic income, projecting its economic and social effects over several years. These insights help decision-makers craft more effective and evidence-based policies.

One of the most powerful aspects of AI-driven political games is their ability to democratize political learning. Traditional political education often requires access to extensive resources, expert lectures, and real-world experience. AI-driven simulations, however, provide an accessible, interactive way for anyone—students, educators, activists, or policymakers—to engage with political decision-making. They bridge the gap between theory and practice, offering a risk-free environment where users can experiment, make mistakes, and learn from their decisions. This hands-on approach fosters a deeper understanding of governance, political strategy, and civic responsibility.

As AI technology continues to evolve, political games will become even more sophisticated, integrating real-time news feeds, social media dynamics, and even AI-generated political personalities that mimic real-world leaders. Future versions could include virtual reality integration, allowing players to experience political negotiations or campaign rallies in a fully immersive environment. The potential for AI-driven political education is vast, and as these tools become more advanced, they will play an increasingly vital role in shaping the next generation of political leaders, analysts, and informed citizens.

AI-driven political games represent a revolutionary approach to political science education. By combining interactivity with real-world complexity, these simulations offer unparalleled insights into policy-making, elections, and international diplomacy. They prepare students not just to understand political systems but to actively engage with them, developing the skills and strategic thinking necessary to navigate the political landscape of the future.

CHAPTER FOUR

The Digital Revolution in Political Science Education

Blended Learning & Online Courses (MOOCs, Coursera, edX, Swayam)

Blended learning and online courses have revolutionized the way political science and related disciplines are taught, making high-quality education accessible to a broader audience. The combination of traditional in-person instruction with online learning resources, often facilitated through platforms like MOOCs (Massive Open Online Courses), Coursera, edX, and Swayam, has created a more flexible and personalized learning experience. This approach allows students to engage with complex political theories, policy debates, and international relations case studies at their own pace while also benefiting from in-depth discussions, mentorship, and real-world applications in physical classrooms or structured online forums.

Blended learning, as a model, enhances traditional education by integrating digital tools and resources with face-to-face interactions. In political science courses, this could mean students watching pre-recorded lectures on comparative politics or international law before attending in-class discussions where they analyze real-world scenarios. This method flips the conventional classroom approach by shifting passive content consumption to online platforms, freeing up classroom time for interactive activities such as debates, simulations, and case studies. For instance, a professor might assign a video lecture on the history of democracy through a MOOC platform like edX and then use class time for a Socratic seminar discussing the strengths and weaknesses of democratic governance in different regions. This dynamic learning approach ensures that students come prepared with foundational knowledge, allowing deeper engagement with course material.

One of the most significant advantages of online courses and MOOCs in political science education is their ability to democratize knowledge. Previously, students had to be physically present at prestigious institutions to access courses taught by leading scholars. Now, platforms like Coursera and Swayam offer courses from universities like Harvard, Yale, and JNU, enabling students worldwide to learn from top political theorists, historians, and policy analysts. These platforms provide structured courses on topics such as electoral systems, public policy analysis, geopolitics, and governance, complete with video lectures, reading materials, interactive quizzes, and peer-reviewed assignments. The ability to earn certificates from recognized institutions also adds value to students' academic and professional credentials, enhancing their career prospects.

MOOCs have also transformed how specialized political science topics are studied. Courses on platforms like FutureLearn and Udemy often focus on niche subjects such as artificial intelligence in politics, global security threats, or environmental diplomacy. This allows learners to tailor their education to their interests and career goals rather than being confined to a rigid university syllabus. Additionally, MOOCs enable interdisciplinary learning, where students can explore connections between political science and fields like economics, sociology, or law. For instance, someone studying governance on Swayam might simultaneously enroll in a Coursera course on behavioral economics to understand voter behavior and policy design better.

Another key aspect of blended learning is its adaptability to different learning styles. Some students grasp concepts better through visual content, making video-based lectures and infographics ideal. Others might prefer reading in-depth reports or engaging in discussion forums where they can exchange perspectives with peers. MOOCs often offer a mix of these formats, catering to diverse learning preferences. Furthermore, these platforms use AI-driven analytics to track learners' progress, offering personalized recommendations for additional resources or topics that need further study. This level of customization makes learning more efficient and engaging.

Blended learning and MOOCs are particularly valuable in professional and continuing education. Many policymakers, government officials, journalists, and activists use online courses to stay updated on the latest political theories, global trends, and policy innovations. For instance, a civil servant preparing for policy reforms might take a Harvard Kennedy School course on governance through edX, while a journalist covering international conflicts might enroll in a MOOC on global diplomacy. These courses provide professionals with the flexibility to learn while working, making it easier to integrate new knowledge into their careers.

Furthermore, the interactive elements of online courses, such as discussion boards, peer-reviewed assignments, and live Q&A sessions, foster a sense of community and collaboration among learners. Political science is inherently a discussion-driven field, and platforms like Coursera and edX often include opportunities for students to engage with professors, experts, and peers from different countries. This global interaction enriches perspectives and helps students understand political phenomena from multiple cultural and ideological viewpoints. For example, a discussion on nationalism in an edX course might include participants from India, the UK, and the United States, leading to a richer debate on how nationalism manifests differently in each context.

Challenges exist in the blended learning model, particularly in ensuring student engagement and motivation in self-paced online courses. Without structured deadlines and in-person accountability, some learners struggle to complete MOOCs. However, many platforms have introduced interactive elements such as gamified quizzes, progress tracking, and group projects to enhance engagement. Moreover, universities integrating MOOCs into their curricula often use a blended approach, requiring students to complete online modules while also participating in guided discussions and assessments in a traditional classroom setting.

Looking ahead, the future of political science education is likely to involve even more integration of blended learning techniques. With advancements in AI, machine learning, and virtual reality, online courses may become more immersive, allowing students to participate in virtual United Nations sessions, policy simulations, or historical reconstructions. Additionally, increased collaboration between universities and MOOC platforms could lead to hybrid degree programs where students combine online coursework with occasional in-person seminars, making higher education more accessible and affordable.

Blended learning and online courses have reshaped how political science is taught and learned, making education more flexible, inclusive, and engaging. Through MOOCs and digital platforms like Coursera, edX, and

Swayam, students and professionals alike can access world-class instruction, tailor their learning experiences, and apply political science theories to real-world challenges. By embracing these modern educational approaches, political science as a discipline can continue to evolve, preparing learners to navigate and shape the complex political landscapes of the future.

Using AI-driven personalized learning tools (adaptive quizzes, chatbots, virtual tutors)

The integration of AI-driven personalized learning tools in political science education has transformed the way students engage with complex political theories, governance models, and global affairs. Adaptive quizzes, chatbots, and virtual tutors have introduced a level of customization and interactivity that traditional education methods often lack. These tools cater to individual learning styles, ensuring that students grasp foundational concepts at their own pace while also challenging them with more advanced analyses when they are ready. By leveraging artificial intelligence, educators can create a more dynamic, responsive, and student-centered learning environment that enhances comprehension and retention.

One of the most impactful AI-driven tools in education is adaptive quizzes. These intelligent assessments analyze a student's responses in real time and adjust the difficulty level accordingly. For example, if a student struggles with questions on the evolution of democracy, the AI system will provide more foundational content, such as the differences between direct and representative democracy, before progressing to complex theories like deliberative democracy. Conversely, if a student demonstrates mastery of a topic, the quiz will introduce more nuanced questions, such as debates on democratic backsliding in modern states. This ensures that students neither feel overwhelmed nor unchallenged, leading to a more efficient and engaging learning process.

Chatbots have also emerged as powerful educational tools, acting as round-the-clock assistants for students studying political science. These AI-powered systems can answer queries, provide explanations, and even guide students through complex subjects with interactive discussions. For instance, a chatbot programmed for international relations might help a student understand real-world applications of balance-of-power theory by offering case studies of Cold War diplomacy. Additionally, these bots can provide reading recommendations, summarize key concepts, and quiz students on past lessons, making self-study more effective. Because chatbots are available anytime, students can receive instant feedback and clarification, reducing the frustration often associated with self-paced learning.

Virtual tutors take AI-driven learning a step further by offering a more personalized and structured approach to education. Unlike static online courses, virtual tutors assess students' progress over time, identifying weak areas and adapting their teaching methods accordingly. A virtual tutor in political science might begin with basic concepts, such as the difference between presidential and parliamentary systems, and then use interactive simulations to demonstrate how these systems function in real-world governance. If a student struggles with understanding electoral processes, the tutor might introduce visual aids, such as infographics of different voting systems, or recommend short explanatory videos. This continuous feedback loop ensures that students not only consume information but also develop a deeper understanding of political structures and ideologies.

One of the most exciting applications of AI-driven personalized learning tools in political science is their ability to facilitate real-time scenario-based learning. Through AI-powered simulations, students can engage in activities such as crafting foreign policy strategies, negotiating international treaties, or analyzing historical conflicts from multiple perspectives. Imagine an AI-driven module where a student takes on the role of a UN diplomat responding to a humanitarian crisis. The virtual tutor provides context, presents challenges, and allows the student to make policy decisions, explaining the consequences of each choice based on historical and theoretical frameworks. Such immersive learning experiences go beyond rote memorization, fostering critical thinking and problem-solving skills essential for political analysis.

Another major advantage of AI-driven education is its ability to make political science more accessible to students from diverse backgrounds. Traditional political science courses often rely heavily on dense academic texts, which can be intimidating for learners who are not accustomed to complex theoretical language. AI tools can simplify content without diluting its essence, breaking down intricate theories into digestible explanations while also offering links to more advanced readings for those who want deeper exploration. Language-processing AI can even translate and localize political science content, allowing students from non-English-speaking regions to engage with high-quality educational materials in their native languages.

AI-driven personalized learning tools also enhance engagement through gamification. By incorporating elements such as leaderboards, achievement badges, and interactive challenges, these tools make learning political science more enjoyable and motivating. For instance, students might compete in a virtual election campaign, where they have to strategize policy positions, manage public relations, and debate opponents—all guided by AI-driven feedback and analysis. This type of experiential learning allows students to understand real-world political dynamics in a way that traditional lectures and textbooks cannot replicate.

Despite these advantages, integrating AI-driven learning tools into political science education does come with challenges. One concern is the potential loss of human interaction, which is crucial for subjects that thrive on debate and discussion. AI can facilitate learning, but it cannot fully replace the nuanced discussions that occur in a lively classroom debate on political ideologies or governance failures. To mitigate this, many educators are combining AI tools with traditional teaching methods, using adaptive quizzes and virtual tutors to reinforce learning while maintaining in-person discussions and collaborative projects.

Another challenge is ensuring that AI-generated content remains unbiased and factually accurate. Political science involves interpreting historical events, policy decisions, and ideological perspectives, and AI systems must be carefully designed to present multiple viewpoints rather than reinforcing existing biases. Developers and educators must work together to continuously refine these tools, ensuring that they provide balanced, well-researched content that encourages critical thinking.

Looking ahead, the role of AI-driven personalized learning tools in political science will likely expand, integrating even more sophisticated technologies such as natural language processing for deeper discussions, augmented reality for immersive historical experiences, and predictive analytics to help students explore future political scenarios. The combination of AI-driven learning and human-led instruction has the potential to create a truly revolutionary educational experience—one where students are not just passive recipients of knowledge but active participants in shaping their political understanding.

AI-driven personalized learning tools such as adaptive quizzes, chatbots, and virtual tutors are transforming political science education by making it more interactive, customized, and accessible. These tools cater to different learning styles, provide real-time feedback, and enhance student engagement through simulations and gamification. While challenges such as maintaining human interaction and ensuring unbiased content remain, the potential benefits of AI in education far outweigh the drawbacks. By leveraging these technologies thoughtfully, political science can be taught in a way that is not only more efficient but also more engaging, empowering students to critically analyze and navigate the complexities of governance, diplomacy, and global affairs.

Digital storytelling & multimedia content in political analysis

Digital storytelling and multimedia content have revolutionized the way political science is taught and understood, making political analysis more engaging, accessible, and impactful. In a world dominated by visual media and rapid information consumption, traditional methods of political education—such as reading dense academic texts or attending long lectures—often struggle to hold the attention of students. Digital storytelling bridges this gap by using videos, interactive graphics, podcasts, and other multimedia formats to bring political concepts to life. By weaving together narratives, visuals, and data, digital storytelling makes political analysis more relatable, fosters deeper understanding, and encourages critical thinking.

One of the most powerful aspects of digital storytelling is its ability to humanize political events and figures. Rather than presenting political science as an abstract subject filled with theories and statistics, multimedia content allows learners to see the human side of governance, activism, and diplomacy. For example, a well-crafted documentary on the Civil Rights Movement does more than just list key events; it immerses the viewer in the struggles, speeches, and emotions of the people who fought for change. Similarly, a video explaining the fall of the Berlin Wall can include firsthand testimonies from those who lived through it, turning a historical event into a personal and emotional experience. These narratives create a stronger emotional connection, making political events more memorable and impactful.

Multimedia content also enhances political analysis by breaking down complex topics into digestible formats. Infographics and data visualizations, for instance, help students grasp intricate political structures, voting patterns, and policy impacts in a visually engaging way. A static paragraph describing income inequality across different countries might be difficult to process, but an interactive map that allows users to compare wealth distribution by region can make the information more accessible. Similarly, animated videos can simplify political ideologies, showing how socialism, capitalism, and liberal democracy function in real-world governance. By presenting information in a structured and visually appealing manner, multimedia content enables learners to absorb and retain key political concepts more effectively.

Podcasts and audio documentaries have also emerged as valuable tools for political storytelling. In-depth discussions with political analysts, historians, and policymakers can provide students with nuanced perspectives on contemporary issues. Unlike traditional lectures, which can sometimes feel rigid, podcasts allow for dynamic conversations where multiple viewpoints are explored. A well-produced political podcast might analyze an election by incorporating expert commentary, interviews with voters, and historical comparisons, providing a richer and more engaging understanding of the political landscape. Additionally, podcasts allow students to consume political content on the go, making learning more flexible and accessible.

Another innovative use of digital storytelling in political analysis is through interactive storytelling platforms and simulations. Websites and applications now allow users to experience political scenarios firsthand, making them active participants rather than passive consumers of information. For example, an interactive simulation might place students in the role of a world leader navigating an international crisis, forcing them to make policy decisions while considering diplomatic, economic, and military consequences. Such experiences help learners understand the complexities of governance and diplomacy in a way that traditional textbooks cannot.

Social media has also become a crucial tool for political storytelling, shaping how narratives are constructed and disseminated. Short-form videos on platforms like YouTube, Instagram, and TikTok have made political education more engaging for younger audiences. A well-crafted explainer video on electoral systems, for instance, can reach millions of viewers, sparking curiosity and discussion about governance and democracy. Similarly, Twitter threads that break down current political events using historical context can make complex issues more understandable to a broader audience. While social media content must be carefully curated to avoid misinformation, it remains a powerful medium for making political analysis more engaging and accessible.

Moreover, digital storytelling is particularly effective in presenting marginalized voices and alternative perspectives that are often overlooked in mainstream political discourse. Traditional political science textbooks tend to focus on dominant narratives, but multimedia content allows for a more inclusive approach. Documentaries, podcasts, and interactive websites can highlight the experiences of indigenous communities, women in politics, grassroots activists, and political movements in the Global South. This ensures that political analysis is not just centered on major world powers but includes diverse voices and perspectives, leading to a more holistic understanding of global politics.

However, while digital storytelling and multimedia content offer many benefits, they also come with challenges. One major concern is the risk of oversimplification. While videos and infographics can make political concepts more accessible, they sometimes lack the depth and nuance that written academic analysis provides. A three-minute video on international relations might give a broad overview of key theories but may not explore the contradictions, debates, and limitations of those theories in sufficient detail. Educators and content creators must strike a balance between making content engaging and ensuring it maintains academic rigor.

Another challenge is the potential for bias and misinformation. In the digital age, political content spreads rapidly, and not all sources are reliable. Some multimedia content may present skewed perspectives, omitting key facts or promoting ideological agendas. It is crucial for learners to develop media literacy skills, enabling them to critically evaluate sources, cross-check information, and differentiate between objective analysis and propaganda. Educators can help by guiding students toward credible multimedia sources and teaching them how to analyze political narratives with a critical eye.

Despite these challenges, digital storytelling and multimedia content have immense potential to revolutionize political science education. By combining narrative techniques with visual and interactive elements, they transform political analysis from a dry academic exercise into a compelling and immersive experience. These tools not only enhance comprehension and retention but also make political education more inclusive and engaging for a diverse audience. As technology continues to evolve, the possibilities for integrating digital storytelling into political science will only expand, opening new doors for innovative teaching methods and deeper public engagement with political issues.

Digital storytelling and multimedia content have become essential tools in modern political analysis, making complex political concepts more engaging, accessible, and emotionally resonant. Whether through documentaries, podcasts, interactive simulations, or social media, these tools help learners connect with political events on a deeper level. While challenges such as oversimplification and misinformation must be addressed, the benefits of using multimedia content in political education far outweigh the drawbacks. As we move into an increasingly digital world, the ability to analyze, interpret, and engage with political content through storytelling will be a crucial skill for both students and citizens alike.

Technology and Data in Political Science

AI, Big Data, and Political Analysis

How AI predicts elections & public opinion trends

Artificial Intelligence (AI) has revolutionized the way elections are analyzed and public opinion is understood. Traditional methods of political forecasting, such as polls and surveys, have long been used to gauge voter sentiment, but they often have limitations in terms of accuracy, sample bias, and real-time adaptability. AI, however, has introduced new levels of precision, speed, and depth in predicting elections and tracking public opinion trends. By leveraging massive datasets, machine learning models, and natural language processing (NLP), AI can analyze voter behavior, social media sentiment, historical trends, and demographic shifts to provide more accurate forecasts and insights into the political landscape.

One of the most powerful applications of AI in election prediction is through big data analysis. AI systems can process vast amounts of structured and unstructured data, including voter demographics, past election results, economic indicators, and campaign strategies. Unlike traditional polling, which relies on a limited number of respondents, AI can analyze millions of data points from diverse sources, making predictions more comprehensive. For instance, machine learning models can examine how different voter groups have responded to economic downturns, policy changes, or political scandals in the past and use that information to forecast future voting behavior. By continuously updating predictions based on new data, AI-driven models can adapt to shifting political dynamics in real time.

Social media has become an essential factor in modern political analysis, and AI plays a crucial role in tracking and interpreting public sentiment across platforms like Twitter, Facebook, and YouTube. Sentiment analysis, a technique powered by natural language processing, allows AI to assess the tone and emotions behind social media posts, comments, and news articles. For example, if a candidate's speech generates a surge of positive mentions online, AI can detect this trend and correlate it with voter enthusiasm. Conversely, if a political scandal leads to a wave of negative comments, AI can quantify the potential damage to a candidate's campaign. This real-time sentiment tracking provides valuable insights that traditional polling methods struggle to capture, particularly in fast-moving election cycles.

Another advanced AI-driven technique used in election prediction is network analysis. By mapping out digital interactions, AI can identify key influencers, opinion leaders, and echo chambers within political discourse. For instance, an AI system can track how political narratives spread across social media, detecting patterns in how certain messages gain traction and influence public opinion. This is particularly useful in understanding the impact of misinformation and propaganda. AI models can detect coordinated efforts to manipulate public sentiment by analyzing bot activity, fake news propagation, and targeted disinformation campaigns. This ability to track the digital landscape gives political analysts a more nuanced understanding of how information flows and affects voter behavior.

AI also enhances traditional polling methods by improving the accuracy of predictive models. Many polling inaccuracies stem from factors such as response bias, low participation rates, and outdated methodologies. AI can refine these models by weighting responses based on real-world demographic distributions and behavioral patterns. For example, if young voters are underrepresented in a survey, AI can adjust the model to reflect their actual voting patterns based on historical data. Additionally, AI can combine multiple sources of data, such as social media trends, economic indicators, and search engine queries, to supplement traditional polling results. This multi-layered approach reduces errors and increases the reliability of election forecasts.

Predictive analytics, another AI-powered technique, allows for the simulation of different electoral scenarios. Political strategists use AI-driven simulations to test how different campaign strategies might impact voter turnout and preferences. By analyzing past elections and voter behavior, AI can generate models that predict the potential effects of campaign messages, policy proposals, or candidate debates. For example, if a political party wants to know how emphasizing economic issues over social issues might affect voter support, AI can run multiple scenarios and provide data-driven insights. This helps campaigns fine-tune their messaging and allocate resources more effectively.

In addition to predicting election outcomes, AI is increasingly being used to analyze public opinion trends over time. Governments, political parties, and researchers use AI to monitor how opinions on key issues evolve, helping policymakers craft strategies that align with public sentiment. For instance, AI-driven public opinion tracking can detect shifts in attitudes toward climate change, immigration, healthcare, or economic policies. By analyzing millions of news articles, opinion pieces, and public statements, AI can identify emerging trends and predict how they might influence future elections.

Despite its advantages, AI-driven election prediction is not without challenges. One major concern is the potential for bias in AI models. If the training data used to build predictive models is biased, the AI's predictions may also be skewed. For example, if an AI model relies heavily on social media data, it may overrepresent the opinions of highly active online users while underrepresenting less digitally engaged populations. Similarly, AI models trained on historical election data may fail to account for unprecedented political shifts or new voting patterns. Ensuring that AI models are trained on diverse and representative datasets is crucial to maintaining accuracy.

Another challenge is the ethical implications of AI in elections. While AI can provide valuable insights, it can also be used to manipulate public opinion through targeted advertising, deepfake videos, and microtargeted propaganda. AI-powered political campaigns can analyze individual voter preferences with remarkable precision, enabling highly personalized messaging. While this can increase voter engagement, it also raises concerns about privacy, misinformation, and potential voter manipulation. Striking a balance between using AI for legitimate political analysis and preventing its misuse is a critical issue that policymakers must address.

Furthermore, the unpredictability of human behavior remains a limitation for AI. Elections are not purely data-driven events; emotions, spontaneous events, and last-minute shifts in public sentiment can have a significant impact on outcomes. AI models may be able to predict trends with high accuracy, but they cannot fully account for unpredictable factors such as political scandals, sudden policy changes, or unexpected voter mobilization efforts. This is why AI should be used as a tool to enhance political analysis rather than as a definitive predictor of election outcomes.

AI has transformed election prediction and public opinion analysis, offering new levels of accuracy, efficiency, and insight. By analyzing vast datasets, tracking social media sentiment, and simulating electoral scenarios, AI helps political analysts, strategists, and policymakers make informed decisions. However, challenges such as bias, ethical concerns, and the unpredictability of human behavior must be carefully managed. While AI is not a perfect predictor, it is an invaluable tool that enhances our understanding of political dynamics and helps navigate the complexities of modern elections. As AI technology continues to evolve, its role in shaping political analysis and forecasting will only grow, making it an essential component of the future of electoral studies.

Data-driven policymaking & real-time political analysis

Data-driven policymaking and real-time political analysis have become indispensable in modern governance. Traditional policymaking often relied on historical data, expert opinions, and slow bureaucratic processes, which sometimes resulted in outdated or ineffective decisions. However, with the advent of big data, artificial intelligence (AI), and real-time analytics, governments and political analysts can now make more informed, precise, and adaptive decisions. This shift towards data-driven policymaking ensures that policies are not only based on evidence but also continuously updated based on real-world developments.

One of the most significant advantages of data-driven policymaking is the ability to process vast amounts of information in real time. Governments now have access to an immense range of data sources, including economic indicators, social media trends, public health statistics, satellite imagery, and even citizen feedback through digital platforms. By analyzing these datasets, policymakers can identify patterns, predict potential crises, and implement timely interventions. For instance, during the COVID-19 pandemic, governments worldwide used real-time data on infection rates, hospital capacities, and mobility patterns to enforce lockdown measures, allocate medical resources, and develop vaccination strategies. Without this data-driven approach, responses would have been slower and less effective.

Another crucial application of data-driven policymaking is in economic governance. Traditionally, economic policies were based on periodic reports and macroeconomic forecasts, which could sometimes lag behind actual developments. Today, AI-driven models can analyze financial transactions, employment data, inflation rates, and consumer behavior in real time, allowing governments to make swift economic decisions. For example, central banks use AI to predict inflation trends and adjust interest rates accordingly. Similarly, tax authorities leverage data analytics to detect fraud and optimize revenue collection. By integrating real-time economic analysis into policymaking, governments can respond more effectively to market fluctuations and financial crises.

Social policies have also benefited from real-time data analysis. AI-powered algorithms can track poverty levels, education rates, healthcare access, and crime statistics across different regions, helping policymakers design targeted interventions. For example, if data analysis shows that a particular district has a high dropout rate among school children, the government can allocate additional resources, improve infrastructure, or launch awareness campaigns to address the issue. Similarly, predictive policing—although controversial—uses crime data to anticipate criminal activity and deploy law enforcement accordingly. While this approach has raised ethical concerns, it demonstrates how real-time data can enhance the effectiveness of public policies.

Environmental policy is another area where data-driven decision-making plays a crucial role. Climate change is a complex issue that requires constant monitoring of variables such as air quality, deforestation rates, ocean temperatures, and carbon emissions. AI-driven climate models analyze these factors to predict extreme weather events, assess the impact of policies, and guide sustainable development strategies. Governments use satellite data to track illegal mining, deforestation, and pollution, enabling timely interventions. For instance, real-time air quality monitoring has led cities to implement emergency measures such as traffic restrictions or factory shutdowns to prevent severe health hazards.

In the realm of public opinion and governance, real-time political analysis has transformed the way leaders interact with citizens. Social media sentiment analysis allows politicians to gauge public reactions to policies, speeches, or global events within minutes. AI algorithms scan millions of tweets, Facebook posts, and news articles to detect shifts in public sentiment, helping policymakers adjust their communication strategies.

During elections, political parties use real-time analytics to refine their campaign messaging, respond to controversies, and mobilize voters more effectively. This level of instant feedback enables leaders to remain connected with their constituencies and adapt to public concerns in real time.

However, data-driven policymaking is not without challenges. One major concern is data privacy and security. Governments collect vast amounts of personal data from citizens, including health records, financial transactions, and social media activity. Ensuring that this data is used responsibly and securely is crucial to maintaining public trust. Additionally, biased data can lead to flawed policymaking. If AI models are trained on incomplete or skewed datasets, they may reinforce existing inequalities instead of solving them. For example, predictive policing algorithms have been criticized for disproportionately targeting certain communities due to biases in historical crime data. Policymakers must therefore be vigilant in ensuring that data-driven decisions are fair, ethical, and transparent.

Another challenge is the risk of over-reliance on data without considering human judgment. While data analytics provides valuable insights, policymaking also requires political, social, and ethical considerations that cannot always be quantified. For example, economic models may suggest cutting public spending to reduce debt, but such measures could negatively impact vulnerable populations. Similarly, AI may recommend policies that are technically efficient but politically unfeasible. Striking a balance between data-driven efficiency and human decision-making is essential to ensure that policies remain both effective and socially acceptable.

Despite these challenges, data-driven policymaking and real-time political analysis are shaping the future of governance. The ability to analyze vast amounts of information in real time allows governments to be more proactive, responsive, and accountable. As technology continues to advance, we can expect even greater integration of AI, big data, and machine learning into policymaking processes. The key to success will be ensuring that these tools are used ethically, transparently, and in a way that benefits society as a whole. By combining data-driven insights with human judgment, policymakers can create more effective, equitable, and forward-thinking solutions to the challenges of the 21st century.

Tools for Data Science in Political Science (Python, R, GIS mapping)

The integration of data science tools in political science has transformed how researchers, policymakers, and analysts study elections, governance, public policy, and international relations. Traditionally, political science relied on qualitative analysis, historical narratives, and surveys to understand political behavior. However, with the rise of big data, artificial intelligence, and machine learning, quantitative analysis has become a crucial component of political research. Tools like Python, R, and Geographic Information Systems (GIS) mapping have emerged as essential for analyzing political trends, voter behavior, policy impact, and even geopolitical dynamics.

Python has gained immense popularity in political science due to its versatility and ease of use. As a programming language, Python offers a wide range of libraries that make it ideal for data analysis, text mining, and machine learning applications in political science. For instance, libraries such as Pandas and NumPy allow researchers to process and analyze large datasets efficiently. This is particularly useful in electoral studies where vast amounts of voter data need to be examined for patterns and trends. Furthermore, Python's Natural Language Processing (NLP) libraries, such as NLTK and spaCy, help analyze political speeches, social media discussions, and news articles to assess sentiment and detect propaganda or misinformation. During election campaigns, parties and political analysts use Python to track voter sentiment in real-time by analyzing tweets, Facebook posts, and online discussions. Such data-driven insights help in adjusting campaign strategies and understanding voter concerns.

Another critical application of Python in political science is network analysis. The study of political networks—whether among political parties, interest groups, or international organizations—has become an essential aspect of political research. Python's NetworkX library allows researchers to visualize and analyze connections between various political actors, revealing insights into influence dynamics, power structures, and coalition formations. For example, by analyzing lobbying networks in the U.S. Congress, researchers can identify which corporations or interest groups have the most influence over legislative decisions. Similarly, in international relations, network analysis can be used to study diplomatic relationships and the influence of global institutions like the United Nations or the

European Union.

While Python is widely used for its general-purpose data science capabilities, R has established itself as a powerful statistical tool in political science research. R is particularly favored for its advanced data visualization and statistical modeling capabilities. Political scientists use R to conduct regression analysis, predictive modeling, and hypothesis testing on political datasets. For example, election forecasting models often rely on R to analyze polling data, economic indicators, and historical voting patterns to predict electoral outcomes. The ggplot2 library in R is especially useful for creating detailed visualizations, such as maps of voting trends, approval ratings over time, and demographic shifts in political preferences.

R is also widely used for survey analysis in political science. Surveys play a crucial role in measuring public opinion, policy preferences, and electoral behavior. The survey package in R helps researchers clean, analyze, and visualize survey data efficiently. Political pollsters, for example, use R to determine the impact of candidates' debates, policy proposals, and media appearances on voter preferences. This statistical rigor allows for more accurate interpretations of public opinion trends, which are essential for both academia and political consulting.

Geographic Information Systems (GIS) mapping has added another dimension to political science research, allowing for spatial analysis of political behavior. GIS technology enables researchers to visualize and analyze geographic data, making it particularly valuable for studies related to electoral geography, political representation, and policy impact. ArcGIS and QGIS are two widely used GIS platforms in political science, but Python and R also offer GIS functionalities through libraries such as Geopandas and sf (in R).

GIS mapping has been instrumental in redistricting and gerrymandering studies. Political scientists use GIS tools to examine how electoral district boundaries influence election outcomes. By overlaying demographic data, voting patterns, and socio-economic indicators, researchers can assess whether district boundaries have been manipulated to favor a particular political party—a practice known as gerrymandering. GIS analysis has played a crucial role in legal cases challenging unfair redistricting practices, providing empirical evidence to support claims of voter suppression or unequal representation.

Beyond electoral studies, GIS mapping is also useful for analyzing policy impact at the regional or national level. For example, researchers studying climate policy can use GIS to map areas most affected by environmental regulations or climate change. Similarly, GIS tools help in studying the distribution of public services, such as healthcare and education, to assess whether government policies are equitably benefiting different regions. By incorporating spatial analysis into political science research, scholars can provide more comprehensive and visually compelling evidence for their findings.

One of the most exciting advancements in data science for political science is the integration of machine learning techniques. Both Python and R offer machine learning frameworks such as Scikit-learn, TensorFlow, and Caret, which enable predictive modeling and classification tasks. Political scientists are increasingly using machine learning to predict election outcomes, analyze legislative behavior, and even detect fake news. For instance, supervised learning models can be trained on historical election data to forecast future voting patterns based on factors such as economic conditions, candidate popularity, and media coverage.

Unsupervised learning techniques, such as clustering, are useful for classifying political actors based on ideological similarity. By analyzing voting records, party manifestos, and public speeches, machine learning models can group politicians or parties based on their policy positions. This helps in understanding political polarization and shifts in ideological alignments over time. Similarly, deep learning models can be used for sentiment analysis, automatically classifying political statements as positive, negative, or neutral, which is particularly useful for media monitoring and campaign strategies.

Despite the numerous advantages of data science tools in political science, there are challenges that researchers must navigate. One major concern is data availability and bias. Political datasets, especially those related to authoritarian regimes or sensitive policy issues, may be difficult to obtain or may contain biases that can distort analysis. Additionally, ethical concerns surrounding the use of AI in political decision-making remain a significant debate. Issues such as algorithmic bias, privacy violations, and misinformation detection require careful consideration to ensure that data science serves democracy rather than undermines it.

The integration of Python, R, and GIS mapping into political science has revolutionized how researchers analyze political behavior, policy effectiveness, and electoral dynamics. These tools provide powerful methods for processing large datasets, visualizing political trends, and making data-driven predictions. As technology continues to evolve, political scientists must adapt to new methodologies while remaining aware of the ethical implications of data-driven research. By leveraging these tools effectively, the field of political science can produce more rigorous, insightful, and impactful analyses that contribute to better governance and public understanding of political systems.

CHAPTER SIX

Social Media and Digital Politics – A Teaching Tool ?

Impact of digital media on democracy (Case studies of Arab Spring, Cambridge Analytica, Indian Elections)

The impact of digital media on democracy has been one of the most transformative yet controversial developments of the 21st century. While digital platforms have enabled greater political participation, activism, and access to information, they have also raised serious concerns about misinformation, data privacy, and manipulation of public opinion. The role of digital media in democratic processes is complex and multifaceted, as it can both empower citizens and be exploited to undermine democratic institutions. To understand this dynamic, three major case studies—The Arab Spring, the Cambridge Analytica scandal, and the role of digital media in Indian elections—offer valuable insights into how digital platforms influence political movements, voter behavior, and governance.

The Arab Spring: Digital Media as a Catalyst for Democratic Movements

The Arab Spring, which began in late 2010, is one of the most powerful examples of how digital media can drive democratic uprisings. It started in Tunisia and quickly spread to Egypt, Libya, Syria, and other parts of the Middle East and North Africa. Social media platforms like Facebook, Twitter, and YouTube played a crucial role in organizing protests, spreading awareness, and mobilizing citizens against authoritarian regimes.

In Tunisia, the self-immolation of Mohamed Bouazizi, a street vendor protesting government corruption, was captured and widely shared on social media, sparking mass protests. Similarly, in Egypt, digital activism played a pivotal role in the 2011 uprising that led to the resignation of President Hosni Mubarak. Platforms like Facebook were used to coordinate protests, with pages such as "We Are All Khaled Said" rallying people against police brutality. Twitter provided real-time updates, allowing activists to communicate and organize despite government crackdowns. YouTube videos showing police violence and large-scale demonstrations garnered global attention, pressuring authoritarian regimes.

Digital media not only facilitated grassroots mobilization but also attracted international support. Hashtags like #Jan25 and #ArabSpring allowed people worldwide to follow developments and express solidarity. However, while digital media helped topple oppressive leaders, it did not necessarily lead to stable democracies. In many cases, authoritarian forces adapted, using digital surveillance, propaganda, and internet shutdowns to suppress dissent. This highlights the dual-edged nature of digital media in democratic struggles—while it can empower citizens, it can also be weaponized by regimes to maintain control.

Cambridge Analytica: The Dark Side of Digital Media in Elections

The Cambridge Analytica scandal revealed the dangers of digital media when used for political manipulation. In 2018, investigative reports exposed how the British political consulting firm Cambridge Analytica harvested data from millions of Facebook users without their consent to create targeted political advertisements. This scandal demonstrated how digital platforms could be used to influence voter behavior through microtargeting and psychological profiling.

Cambridge Analytica used Facebook data to build detailed psychological profiles of voters in the United States and the United Kingdom. By analyzing users' likes, comments, and online behavior, they categorized individuals into personality types and tailored political messages accordingly. This microtargeting technique was particularly influential in the 2016 U.S. presidential election and the Brexit referendum.

The key issue in this case was the ethical misuse of personal data. Users were unaware that their online activities were being tracked and exploited for political advertising. This raised serious concerns about privacy, consent, and the ability of digital platforms to manipulate democratic processes. The scandal led to widespread debates about data protection, prompting stricter regulations like the General Data Protection Regulation (GDPR) in the European Union.

Beyond Cambridge Analytica, the incident highlighted broader concerns about the role of digital media in shaping public opinion. Social media algorithms prioritize sensational and polarizing content, often amplifying misinformation and extremist views. This has led to increased political polarization and the spread of fake news, eroding trust in democratic institutions. The scandal underscored the need for transparency in digital political advertising and greater accountability from tech companies in safeguarding democracy.

Indian Elections: Digital Media as a Political Battleground

India, the world's largest democracy, has witnessed a dramatic shift in electoral campaigns due to the rise of digital media. With over 800 million internet users, India has become a digital battleground where political parties leverage social media, data analytics, and online propaganda to influence voters.

During the 2014 and 2019 general elections, digital media played a central role in shaping political discourse. Political parties used Facebook, Twitter, WhatsApp, and YouTube to reach millions of voters. Narendra Modi's Bharatiya Janata Party (BJP) emerged as a pioneer in digital campaigning, using data-driven strategies, targeted advertisements, and WhatsApp groups to mobilize supporters. The party's IT cell created a vast network of influencers, social media warriors, and content creators to push its narrative.

One of the most striking aspects of digital media in Indian elections is the spread of misinformation. WhatsApp, the most widely used messaging app in India, has been a major source of fake news and propaganda. In several instances, misinformation campaigns have influenced voter perception, leading to communal tensions and political polarization. For example, doctored videos, false statistics, and misleading news articles have been used to create divisions and manipulate public opinion. The Election Commission of India has struggled to regulate the flood of misinformation, highlighting the challenges of maintaining electoral integrity in the digital age.

However, digital media has also democratized political participation. It has enabled smaller parties and independent candidates to reach voters without the need for expensive traditional campaigns. Platforms like Twitter have allowed direct engagement between politicians and citizens, making political discourse more interactive. Civil society organizations and fact-checking groups have also used digital tools to counter misinformation and promote voter awareness.

The Indian elections illustrate how digital media can both strengthen and weaken democracy. While it enhances political engagement and accessibility, it also poses significant risks in terms of misinformation, privacy violations, and the potential for mass manipulation.

Balancing the Power of Digital Media in Democracy

The three case studies—the Arab Spring, Cambridge Analytica, and Indian elections—demonstrate that digital media is neither inherently good nor bad for democracy. Its impact depends on how it is used and regulated. On one hand, digital media can empower citizens, facilitate political movements, and enhance democratic participation. On the other hand, it can be exploited for propaganda, misinformation, and data manipulation, threatening the very foundations of democracy.

To mitigate the negative effects of digital media, governments and tech companies must adopt responsible policies. Strengthening data privacy laws, increasing transparency in political advertising, and promoting digital literacy are crucial steps toward ensuring that digital platforms serve democracy rather than undermine it. Fact-checking initiatives and independent media organizations must be supported to counter misinformation effectively. Additionally, platforms like Facebook, Twitter, and WhatsApp must take greater responsibility for curbing fake news and preventing the misuse of their algorithms for political gain.

Ultimately, the future of digital media and democracy will depend on how societies adapt to these challenges. Citizens must become more critical consumers of digital content, policymakers must enforce ethical regulations, and technology companies must prioritize democratic values over profit. Only through collective effort can digital media truly become a force for strengthening, rather than weakening, democratic institutions worldwide.

Teaching students to analyze online propaganda & misinformation

In an age where information is just a click away, the ability to critically analyze online content is more important than ever. The internet has transformed how we consume news, shaping our perceptions of politics, history, and society. However, with this vast access to information comes an overwhelming flood of propaganda, misinformation, and outright falsehoods. Many students today rely on social media and digital platforms for news, often encountering manipulated narratives designed to mislead or provoke emotional reactions. Teaching them how to recognize, evaluate, and respond to misinformation is essential, not just for academic purposes but for their role as informed citizens. It is not enough to tell them what is true and what is false; they must develop the skills to assess credibility on their own.

One of the first steps in combating misinformation is understanding how and why it spreads. Propaganda is not a new concept—it has been used throughout history to shape public opinion, from wartime posters to political campaigns. However, the digital age has given propaganda an unprecedented reach. Social media algorithms prioritize engagement, meaning that sensationalized and misleading content often spreads faster than factual reporting. False stories are shared not just by bots or malicious actors but by everyday users who may not realize they are spreading misinformation. Teaching students about the mechanics behind viral hoaxes, deepfake videos, and politically motivated fake news helps them recognize these patterns in real time. They need to understand that just because something appears frequently on their feed does not mean it is true.

A crucial skill in analyzing online information is recognizing bias and manipulation techniques. Every source has a perspective, and students must learn to question the intent behind the content they consume. Who is the author? What is their background? Is the information supported by credible sources, or is it based on opinion and selective data? Many misinformation campaigns use emotionally charged language to bypass rational thinking, making readers feel anger, fear, or outrage before they have a chance to critically evaluate the facts. By analyzing real-world examples—such as misleading headlines, out-of-context quotes, and deceptive statistics—students can develop an instinct for identifying red flags in online content. They must learn to ask, "Who benefits from this narrative?" and "What is missing from this story?"

Beyond awareness, students need practical tools to verify information. Fact-checking websites such as Snopes, FactCheck.org, and Alt News provide valuable resources, but students must also develop independent verification skills. Reverse image search tools help identify whether a viral photo has been taken out of context or digitally altered. Analyzing URLs and website credibility can reveal whether a source is legitimate or part of a network of misinformation. AI-generated deepfake videos, which can convincingly fake speeches or interviews, require a critical eye to detect inconsistencies in facial expressions, unnatural voice modulations, or lighting mismatches. Recognizing these digital tricks takes practice, but with guidance, students can learn to navigate the online world with confidence.

Encouraging open discussions about misinformation is just as important as providing the tools to detect it. Classrooms should be spaces where students feel comfortable questioning sources, debating different viewpoints, and dissecting how narratives are constructed. Instead of simply telling students what to believe, educators should engage them in active media analysis. A news article could be dissected sentence by sentence to examine its framing, or students could be challenged to trace the origins of a viral claim. Role-playing exercises, where students take on the perspectives of journalists, politicians, or fact-checkers, can help them understand how information is shaped before it reaches the public. The goal is to create a habit of critical thinking—so that when students encounter dubious claims outside the classroom, their first instinct is to question and verify rather than accept and share.

Real-world case studies make these lessons tangible. The misinformation surrounding the COVID-19 pandemic, for example, is a powerful case study in how false medical advice, conspiracy theories, and politically motivated distortions spread online. The 2016 Cambridge Analytica scandal revealed how social media data was weaponized to manipulate voter behavior, demonstrating the intersection of misinformation and political strategy. The Arab Spring showed both the power and dangers of digital activism, where social media played a crucial role in mobilizing protests but was also used to spread false narratives. Analyzing such cases helps students see the real impact of misinformation, making them more cautious and responsible media consumers.

Teaching students to analyze online propaganda and misinformation is not just about protecting them from being misled—it is about empowering them to engage with the world thoughtfully. In a society where digital literacy is as important as traditional literacy, these skills are fundamental to navigating modern life. By fostering skepticism without cynicism, curiosity without gullibility, and awareness without fear, we prepare students to be informed citizens in a rapidly changing information landscape. If they can learn to think critically about the stories they encounter, they will be less susceptible to manipulation and better equipped to contribute to meaningful discussions, both online and in real life.

Developing media literacy skills for political analysis

In an age where political discourse is shaped by digital media, developing media literacy skills is essential for anyone seeking to analyze political events critically. The overwhelming amount of information available online—ranging from reliable journalism to outright propaganda—requires individuals to distinguish between fact and manipulation. Media literacy in political analysis is not just about consuming news; it is about questioning sources, identifying biases, verifying information, and understanding the broader context in which political narratives are constructed. Without these skills, people are vulnerable to misinformation, emotional manipulation, and ideological echo chambers that reinforce pre-existing beliefs rather than challenge them.

One of the first steps in developing media literacy for political analysis is recognizing the different types of media sources and their credibility. Traditional news outlets, independent journalism platforms, government sources, think tanks, academic research, and social media all play a role in shaping political narratives, but not all are equally reliable. Students and political analysts must learn to assess the credibility of a source by looking at its ownership, funding, history, and editorial policies. For instance, understanding whether a media outlet is state-controlled, corporate-funded, or independently operated can reveal potential biases in its reporting. Similarly, distinguishing between opinion pieces, investigative journalism, and propaganda helps readers contextualize the information they receive.

Another critical skill is understanding media bias and framing. Every news article, video, or social media post presents information from a certain angle, influenced by cultural, political, and economic factors. The way a political event is reported can vary dramatically depending on the source. For example, coverage of protests, elections, or international conflicts may differ between left-leaning and right-leaning media outlets. Learning to analyze how headlines are written, what language is used, and which facts are emphasized or omitted can reveal underlying biases. By comparing multiple sources on the same topic, students can identify patterns and assess how different narratives are constructed.

Fact-checking and verification are fundamental aspects of media literacy. In political analysis, false or misleading information can spread rapidly, influencing public opinion and even policy decisions. Knowing how to verify claims through independent fact-checking websites, cross-referencing multiple reputable sources, and consulting primary documents—such as government reports, official statements, and academic studies—helps ensure accuracy. Moreover, students should be trained to detect misinformation tactics such as deepfake videos, doctored images, and misleading statistics. Political campaigns, advocacy groups, and even foreign actors have used such tactics to manipulate perceptions and sway elections.

Social media has become a primary battleground for political discourse, making digital literacy an essential component of political media analysis. Algorithms on platforms like Twitter, Facebook, and YouTube prioritize content that generates engagement, often amplifying sensationalized or polarizing narratives. Understanding how these algorithms work allows individuals to recognize when they are being steered toward biased or emotionally charged content. Additionally, students must learn to identify coordinated disinformation campaigns, troll farms, and bot activity, which are frequently used to manipulate public perception.

Beyond critical consumption, media literacy also involves ethical engagement. As digital citizens, individuals must be aware of the consequences of sharing unverified or misleading information. Encouraging responsible discussion, fact-based arguments, and respectful debate is crucial in fostering a well-informed public. Political analysts, educators, and students should strive to challenge misinformation not through aggressive confrontation but through rational discussion and evidence-based arguments.

Ultimately, developing media literacy skills for political analysis empowers individuals to navigate the complex information landscape with confidence. It enables them to separate truth from propaganda, engage in meaningful discussions, and contribute to a more informed society. In a world where political narratives are increasingly shaped by digital media, the ability to think critically, question assumptions, and verify information is not just an academic skill—it is a democratic necessity.

CHAPTER SEVEN

Cybersecurity, Digital Diplomacy, and the Future of International Relations

The rise of cyber warfare & its impact on global politics

The rise of cyber warfare has transformed the landscape of global politics, introducing new forms of conflict, power struggles, and security challenges. Unlike traditional warfare, where battles are fought on land, sea, or air, cyber warfare operates in the digital realm, targeting critical infrastructure, government networks, financial systems, and even public opinion. This shift has redefined national security, making cybersecurity as crucial as military defense. As states, non-state actors, and criminal organizations develop advanced cyber capabilities, the geopolitical balance of power is increasingly being influenced by digital conflicts rather than conventional military engagements.

One of the most significant aspects of cyber warfare is its ability to disrupt a nation's infrastructure without direct physical confrontation. State-sponsored cyberattacks have targeted power grids, communication networks, and financial institutions, causing large-scale economic and political instability. For example, the 2010 Stuxnet attack on Iran's nuclear facilities, allegedly carried out by the United States and Israel, demonstrated how cyber warfare could cripple a nation's strategic assets without launching a single missile. Similarly, Russia's cyberattacks on Ukraine, targeting government websites, banks, and energy grids, have highlighted how cyber warfare is used alongside conventional military tactics in hybrid warfare.

Cyber warfare is not just about attacking infrastructure—it is also a powerful tool for influencing public opinion and political processes. The manipulation of social media, hacking of political campaigns, and spread of disinformation have become central strategies in modern cyber conflicts. The 2016 U.S. presidential election saw allegations of Russian interference through hacking and propaganda campaigns designed to sway public sentiment. Similar tactics have been observed in elections across Europe, Asia, and Africa, where cyber operatives work to influence voter behavior, spread false narratives, and undermine democratic institutions. The ability to control digital information has given rise to a new form of power where states can shape political outcomes in rival nations without traditional forms of intervention.

Beyond state actors, cyber warfare has also empowered non-state groups, including terrorist organizations, hacktivists, and cybercriminals. Groups like Anonymous have carried out cyberattacks on governments and corporations to push political agendas, while extremist organizations use encrypted messaging apps and dark web platforms for recruitment and propaganda. Ransomware attacks, where hackers demand payment to restore access to critical systems, have also emerged as a significant threat, affecting both public and private sector institutions. The WannaCry ransomware attack of 2017, which affected hospitals, banks, and businesses across 150 countries, demonstrated the global reach and devastating consequences of cybercrime.

The growing dependence on digital technology has made cyber security a top priority for nations worldwide. Governments are investing heavily in cybersecurity measures, establishing dedicated cyber defense units, and enacting strict data protection laws. Countries like the United States, China, and Russia have developed sophisticated cyber command centers capable of launching and defending against digital attacks. International organizations, including NATO and the United Nations, have also recognized cyber warfare as a major security threat, leading to discussions on creating global norms and regulations for cyber conflicts. However, enforcing such regulations remains a challenge, as cyber operations are often carried out covertly, making it difficult to attribute responsibility or hold perpetrators accountable.

The rise of cyber warfare has also intensified geopolitical rivalries, leading to what some experts call a "cyber arms race." Nations are competing to develop advanced cyber weapons, artificial intelligence-driven hacking tools, and quantum computing capabilities that could break existing encryption systems. The lack of clear international laws governing cyber warfare has further escalated tensions, as countries engage in espionage, data theft, and cyber sabotage without fear of direct retaliation. The ongoing U.S.-China technology rivalry, centered around cybersecurity concerns, intellectual property theft, and 5G infrastructure, is a prime example of how cyber capabilities are shaping global power dynamics.

As cyber warfare continues to evolve, the need for international cooperation and regulation becomes more urgent. Cyber conflicts do not respect national borders, and a single attack can have ripple effects across multiple nations. The challenge lies in balancing national security interests with the need for digital freedom and privacy. While governments push for stricter cybersecurity laws, there is also growing concern over mass surveillance and the erosion of individual freedoms in the name of national security. The future of cyber warfare will likely involve not only technological advancements but also ethical and legal debates on how to manage digital conflicts in a globally interconnected world.

In this new era of cyber warfare, global politics is no longer defined solely by military strength or economic power. Nations that dominate the digital battlefield hold the advantage in shaping international relations, influencing domestic affairs, and defending against emerging threats. As technology continues to advance, the impact of cyber warfare on global politics will only deepen, making cybersecurity one of the most critical issues of the 21st century.

Social media diplomacy (Twiplomacy) and global negotiations

The rise of social media has revolutionized the way diplomacy and international negotiations are conducted. In the digital era, traditional diplomatic channels—characterized by private discussions, official statements, and controlled press releases—are increasingly being supplemented, and at times replaced, by real-time communication on platforms like Twitter, Facebook, and LinkedIn. This phenomenon, often referred to as "Twiplomacy" (Twitter Diplomacy), has transformed the way global leaders, foreign ministries, and international organizations engage with each other and with the public. It has introduced new opportunities for transparency, engagement, and rapid response, but it has also brought challenges related to misinformation, misinterpretation, and the erosion of formal diplomatic protocols.

One of the most significant advantages of social media diplomacy is its ability to foster direct and immediate communication between global leaders. Unlike traditional diplomatic statements that are filtered through bureaucratic processes, a tweet or a post from a head of state can instantly reach millions of people worldwide. This direct engagement allows leaders to set the narrative, respond quickly to crises, and demonstrate political resolve without relying on traditional media channels. A prominent example is how former U.S. President Donald Trump used Twitter to communicate foreign policy positions, threaten adversaries, and negotiate trade deals in real-time. Similarly, Indian Prime Minister Narendra Modi, French President Emmanuel Macron, and Ukrainian President Volodymyr Zelenskyy have leveraged social media to shape international perceptions and mobilize support for their policies.

Social media has also become a crucial tool for public diplomacy—engaging not only with other governments but also with global audiences. Foreign ministries, embassies, and international organizations use social media to communicate policy positions, counter misinformation, and build relationships with foreign publics. This form of digital diplomacy has been particularly effective in crisis situations. For instance, during Russia's invasion of Ukraine in 2022, Ukrainian officials used Twitter and Telegram to rally international support, expose war crimes, and coordinate humanitarian aid. The ability to bypass traditional media and speak directly to global audiences has made social media an indispensable tool for shaping international opinion.

In global negotiations, social media plays a dual role—it can both facilitate dialogue and complicate delicate diplomatic processes. On one hand, it has made diplomacy more transparent by allowing the public to follow key developments in international talks, such as climate summits, trade agreements, and nuclear negotiations. Hashtags like #COP26, #IranDeal, and #G7Summit have enabled citizens, activists, and journalists to engage with and influence negotiations in ways that were previously impossible. On the other hand, the public nature of social media can make diplomacy more challenging, as negotiators must carefully balance official statements with the expectations of their domestic and international audiences. A poorly worded tweet or a leaked conversation can derail negotiations, escalate tensions, and even trigger conflicts.

One of the biggest risks of social media diplomacy is the spread of misinformation and propaganda. In an age where state-sponsored disinformation campaigns are widespread, governments and political actors use social media to manipulate narratives, spread falsehoods, and undermine rivals. For example, during the COVID-19 pandemic, misinformation about vaccines and public health policies was weaponized by different state and non-state actors to discredit opponents and sow distrust in international institutions. Similarly, in geopolitical conflicts, social media has been used to spread doctored images, fake news, and conspiracy theories to influence public opinion and destabilize governments.

Another challenge is the loss of nuance in diplomatic communication. Traditional diplomatic language is carefully crafted to avoid escalation and to leave room for negotiation. In contrast, social media platforms encourage brevity, informality, and sensationalism—traits that can be counterproductive in high-stakes international relations. For example, when two rival nations exchange provocative tweets, it can lead to unnecessary tensions or misinterpretations that make formal negotiations more difficult. The 2018 Twitter exchanges between the U.S. and North Korea, where leaders traded threats of nuclear war, illustrate how social media diplomacy can sometimes escalate rather than resolve conflicts.

Despite these challenges, social media diplomacy is here to stay, and governments are continuously adapting to its evolving role in global affairs. Many countries have established dedicated digital diplomacy teams within their foreign ministries to manage their online presence strategically. Training programs for diplomats now include courses on digital engagement, cybersecurity, and social media analytics. In addition, artificial intelligence (AI) and big data analytics are being used to track global sentiment, detect disinformation campaigns, and assess the impact of digital diplomacy efforts.

Looking ahead, the future of social media diplomacy will likely be shaped by emerging technologies such as AI-generated content, deepfake videos, and virtual reality diplomacy. As digital communication continues to evolve, governments must find ways to leverage these tools for constructive engagement while mitigating the risks associated with misinformation, cyber warfare, and diplomatic missteps. Ultimately, the effectiveness of social media diplomacy will depend on how well it is integrated with traditional diplomatic strategies to enhance global negotiations and foster meaningful international cooperation.

The role of blockchain in elections & digital governance

In the modern era, ensuring transparency, security, and efficiency in elections and governance has become a global challenge. With the rise of cyber threats, electoral fraud, and concerns over the integrity of democratic processes, blockchain technology has emerged as a potential game-changer. Blockchain, a decentralized and tamper-proof ledger system, offers a revolutionary approach to elections and digital governance by enhancing transparency, security, and trust in public administration. From securing voter identities to enabling real-time verification of votes, blockchain has the potential to reshape how democratic institutions function in the digital age.

One of the most pressing concerns in elections worldwide is voter fraud and electoral manipulation. Traditional voting systems, whether paper-based or electronic, have inherent vulnerabilities that can be exploited through hacking, coercion, or administrative errors. Blockchain can provide a robust solution by offering a decentralized and immutable record of votes. When a vote is cast using blockchain, it is securely encrypted and stored in a distributed ledger that cannot be altered or deleted. This ensures that once a vote is recorded, it remains tamper-proof, eliminating concerns over ballot stuffing, vote deletion, or unauthorized alterations.

Moreover, blockchain-based voting systems can enhance voter accessibility and participation. In many countries, voter turnout remains low due to logistical challenges, long queues, or lack of access to polling stations. Blockchain-enabled online voting systems can allow citizens to cast their votes securely from anywhere in the world using their smartphones or computers. This is particularly beneficial for expatriates, military personnel stationed abroad, and people with disabilities who face difficulties reaching polling stations. By ensuring secure remote voting, blockchain can help improve democratic participation and inclusivity.

Beyond elections, blockchain plays a critical role in strengthening digital governance. Governments handle vast amounts of sensitive data related to citizens, public policies, and financial transactions. However, traditional data management systems are often centralized, making them susceptible to cyberattacks, data breaches, and corruption. Blockchain provides a decentralized alternative that ensures data integrity, security, and transparency. For example, land records, birth certificates, business registrations, and social welfare distributions can be securely stored on blockchain networks, reducing bureaucratic inefficiencies and preventing fraudulent practices.

One of the key applications of blockchain in governance is digital identity verification. Currently, identity fraud and data theft pose significant challenges in both public and private sectors. Blockchain-based digital IDs can offer citizens a secure and verifiable identity that can be used for various government services, from applying for passports to accessing healthcare benefits. Countries like Estonia have already implemented blockchain-based e-governance systems, allowing citizens to securely access services online without the risk of identity theft. Such systems reduce the reliance on physical documents and minimize the risk of corruption associated with manual verification processes.

Furthermore, blockchain enhances government accountability and transparency. Public trust in government institutions often erodes due to opaque decision-making, corruption, and lack of access to information. By using blockchain, governments can create public ledgers where financial transactions, budget allocations, and policy decisions are recorded in a transparent and immutable manner. Citizens can track government spending in real time, ensuring that public funds are used efficiently and ethically. For instance, some countries have started using blockchain to track foreign aid distribution, ensuring that funds reach the intended beneficiaries without mismanagement or corruption.

However, despite its potential, the adoption of blockchain in elections and governance comes with challenges. One major concern is the issue of scalability. Managing a national election on a blockchain network requires high computational power and efficient data processing, which can be complex and resource-intensive. Additionally, cybersecurity threats such as 51% attacks—where a group of malicious actors gains control of the blockchain network—pose risks to the integrity of the system. Governments must invest in robust security measures and regulatory frameworks to mitigate these risks and ensure the credibility of blockchain-based governance solutions.

Another challenge is public trust and digital literacy. Many citizens are unfamiliar with blockchain technology and may be skeptical about using it for critical democratic processes like elections. Educating the public on how blockchain works and ensuring a user-friendly experience are essential steps for widespread adoption. Governments must also address legal and ethical concerns related to privacy and data protection while implementing blockchain-based solutions.

Despite these challenges, blockchain continues to gain traction in electoral processes and governance worldwide. Several pilot projects have already demonstrated its effectiveness. For instance, in the 2018 midterm elections in the United States, West Virginia experimented with blockchain-based voting for overseas military personnel. Similarly, countries like Switzerland and Ukraine have conducted blockchain voting trials to explore its feasibility for national elections. While large-scale adoption may take time, these initiatives highlight the growing interest in leveraging blockchain to strengthen democratic institutions.

Looking ahead, the integration of blockchain with artificial intelligence (AI) and smart contracts could further enhance digital governance. Smart contracts, self-executing agreements coded into blockchain networks, can automate various government processes such as tax collection, social security distribution, and public procurement. By reducing human intervention and bureaucratic inefficiencies, blockchain-powered governance can pave the way for more efficient, transparent, and accountable public administration.

Ultimately, the role of blockchain in elections and digital governance represents a paradigm shift in how societies ensure fairness, security, and trust in democratic institutions. While challenges remain, continued research, investment, and policy innovation can help harness the full potential of blockchain to build resilient and inclusive governance systems for the future.

Interdisciplinary Approaches in Political Science Education

CHAPTER EIGHT

Political Science and Behavioral Economics

Understanding voter behavior using psychology & economics

Voter behavior is a complex phenomenon shaped by a combination of psychological and economic factors. The decision to vote, whom to vote for, and how individuals perceive political candidates and policies are deeply influenced by cognitive biases, social influences, personal experiences, and economic conditions. By examining voter behavior through the lenses of psychology and economics, we can better understand what drives people to participate in elections, how they form political opinions, and why electoral outcomes often defy traditional rational models.

Psychologically, voting is not just a rational calculation but also an emotional and social act. One of the key psychological theories that explain voter behavior is prospect theory, which suggests that people evaluate political choices based on perceived gains and losses rather than absolute outcomes. For example, a voter who has lost a job due to an economic downturn may be more likely to vote for a candidate promising economic reform, even if they are uncertain about the effectiveness of that candidate's policies. Loss aversion—a principle of behavioral psychology—suggests that people tend to weigh potential losses more heavily than equivalent gains. This means that voters are more likely to react strongly to negative campaign messages, such as warnings about economic collapse or threats to social stability, rather than positive messages about future progress.

Another important psychological concept is confirmation bias, where individuals seek information that aligns with their preexisting beliefs and ignore evidence that contradicts them. In the age of digital media, this bias is reinforced by algorithm-driven news feeds that expose people to partisan content, creating ideological echo chambers. This has significant implications for voter behavior, as it leads to political polarization and reduces openness to alternative perspectives. Political campaigns and parties leverage this psychological tendency by using targeted advertisements and rhetoric that reinforce existing loyalties rather than persuading undecided voters.

Social identity theory also plays a crucial role in voting behavior. People often identify with political parties or movements in the same way they identify with cultural or religious groups. This means that voting is not always about policy preferences but about group loyalty and identity. For instance, someone who identifies strongly as a conservative or liberal may support their party's candidate regardless of specific policy positions, simply because they see it as an extension of their personal identity. This explains why some voters remain loyal to political parties even when their economic circumstances worsen or when the party's policies change significantly over time.

Beyond psychology, economics provides valuable insights into voter behavior, particularly through the concept of rational choice theory. This theory suggests that individuals make voting decisions by weighing the costs and benefits of different candidates and policies. However, real-world voter behavior often deviates from this model because of factors like misinformation, limited information, and emotional biases. Economists argue that many voters engage in retrospective voting, meaning they base their decisions on past economic performance rather than future policy proposals. For example, an incumbent government is more likely to be re-elected if economic conditions have improved during its tenure, even if the opposition party presents better long-term economic policies.

Another economic theory relevant to voter behavior is public choice theory, which applies economic principles to political decision-making. It suggests that politicians and voters act in self-interest, with voters supporting candidates who promise direct benefits such as tax cuts, subsidies, or job creation programs. This is why populist policies—such as debt forgiveness, free healthcare, or cash transfers—often gain traction during election cycles, even if they are economically unsustainable in the long run.

Income inequality and economic instability also shape voter preferences. In times of economic downturn, voters tend to favor government intervention, leading to greater support for left-leaning or progressive candidates who promise wealth redistribution and stronger social safety nets. Conversely, during periods of economic growth, voters may lean towards conservative policies that promote deregulation and free-market principles. The 2008 global financial crisis, for instance, led to a political shift in many countries, with voters supporting leaders who promised economic reform and regulation of financial markets.

Behavioral economics further challenges the idea that voters always act rationally. The paradox of voting suggests that, from a purely economic standpoint, the cost of voting (such as time, effort, and transportation) often outweighs the individual impact of a single vote. Yet, millions of people still participate in elections. This paradox is explained by factors like civic duty, social pressure, and emotional engagement. Studies have shown that when people are reminded of their responsibility as citizens or when they believe that others in their community are voting, they are more likely to turn out to vote. This is why voter mobilization campaigns, including messages like "Your vote matters" or "Be a responsible citizen," are effective in increasing turnout.

One of the most intriguing aspects of voter behavior is herd mentality, where people vote based on the influence of their peers, family, or community rather than independent reasoning. This explains why voter preferences often cluster geographically, with entire neighborhoods or regions leaning towards a particular party. Political campaigns capitalize on this by targeting influential figures in local communities who can sway large groups of voters. Similarly, the bandwagon effect—where people support a candidate simply because they appear to be winning—plays a significant role in shaping election outcomes. When media outlets report on polling trends showing a candidate in the lead, undecided voters may be more inclined to vote for that candidate to align with the majority.

Understanding voter behavior through psychology and economics is particularly important in today's digital age, where political campaigns use sophisticated data analytics to influence decisions. Micro-targeting, driven by artificial intelligence and big data, allows campaigns to predict voter preferences and tailor messages accordingly. By analyzing online behavior, economic status, and psychological profiles, political strategists can craft personalized advertisements that appeal to an individual's specific fears, aspirations, or biases.

Voter behavior is shaped by a complex interplay of psychological biases, social influences, and economic conditions. While traditional economic models assume that voters make rational decisions based on self-interest, psychological insights reveal that emotions, identity, and cognitive biases often override logical reasoning. Understanding these factors not only helps explain past election outcomes but also provides valuable lessons for political strategists, policymakers, and educators. As technology and data-driven politics continue to evolve, the ability to analyze voter behavior using psychology and economics will become increasingly crucial in shaping democratic processes and governance.

Nudging & Behavioral Policy Tools (Richard Thaler's Nudge Theory)

In the realm of public policy and governance, traditional approaches often rely on regulations, financial incentives, or direct interventions to influence behavior. However, behavioral economics introduces a more subtle yet effective method—nudging. Popularized by Nobel laureate Richard Thaler and Cass Sunstein in their book Nudge: Improving Decisions About Health, Wealth, and Happiness, the concept of nudging suggests that small, carefully designed changes in the way choices are presented can significantly influence people's decisions without restricting their freedom. Unlike coercion or mandates, nudging leverages insights from psychology and behavioral economics to steer individuals toward better choices while preserving their autonomy.

At the heart of nudge theory is the understanding that human decision-making is often irrational. Traditional economic models assume that people make logical, self-interested choices based on available information. However, behavioral economics reveals that cognitive biases, habits, and social influences frequently lead individuals to make suboptimal decisions. For instance, people tend to procrastinate, overvalue immediate gratification, and struggle with complex choices. Nudging helps counteract these biases by designing policies and environments that make desirable behaviors easier and more appealing.

One of the most famous applications of nudge theory is in retirement savings. Many employees fail to enroll in retirement plans due to inertia or the complexity of financial decisions. Instead of mandating participation, policymakers in several countries introduced automatic enrollment—a nudge that makes saving the default option while allowing employees to opt out if they wish. This simple change has dramatically increased participation rates, demonstrating how adjusting the default setting can lead to better outcomes without restricting personal choice.

Another widely recognized example is the use of opt-out organ donation systems. In countries where individuals must actively sign up to become organ donors, participation rates are low due to inaction or procrastination. However, in countries where people are automatically enrolled as donors unless they choose to opt out, the rates are significantly higher. This demonstrates the power of the status quo bias—people tend to stick with the default option rather than making an active choice, even when the stakes are high.

Public health policies have also benefited from nudging strategies. For instance, placing healthier food options at eye level in supermarkets or school cafeterias increases the likelihood of people choosing nutritious meals without restricting access to less healthy alternatives. Similarly, the use of social norm messaging—such as informing individuals that "90% of your neighbors pay their taxes on time"—has been shown to improve tax compliance rates. People are highly influenced by what they perceive as common behavior, and presenting information in a way that highlights positive social norms encourages adherence to beneficial practices.

Nudge theory has been particularly effective in encouraging environmentally friendly behaviors. Simple interventions like adding a small green light to electric vehicle charging stations to indicate when they are using renewable energy can subtly encourage drivers to charge their vehicles at optimal times. Similarly, energy bills that compare a household's energy consumption to that of its more efficient neighbors can motivate individuals to reduce their usage. These strategies rely on the principle of comparative feedback, where people adjust their behavior when they see themselves lagging behind social norms.

In governance and political engagement, nudging has been used to increase voter turnout. Studies have shown that sending personalized messages reminding citizens of their civic duty or informing them that their participation will be recorded (without violating privacy) can significantly boost voting rates. One experiment found that simply rewording a message from "Election Day is coming up" to "You are a voter. Election Day is coming up" increased participation. This minor linguistic shift reinforces a person's identity as a voter, making them more likely to act accordingly.

Digital platforms have also incorporated nudge-based strategies to improve user engagement and decision-making. Governments and tech companies use behavioral insights to design user interfaces that promote beneficial actions, such as reducing screen time, managing online privacy settings, or making informed financial choices. For instance, social media platforms have introduced prompts that ask users, "Are you sure you want to share this article?" if they attempt to post content without reading it—helping to curb the spread of misinformation.

Despite its successes, nudging is not without criticism. Some argue that it can be manipulative, subtly guiding people toward choices they might not have made otherwise. Ethical concerns arise when nudges serve commercial or political interests rather than public well-being. Critics also point out that not all nudges are equally effective across different cultural and socio-economic groups. A nudge that works in a Western democracy may not necessarily yield the same results in a developing nation with different social and economic structures.

Moreover, nudging alone is not a substitute for structural policy changes. While nudges can help individuals make better choices, they cannot address deep-rooted systemic issues like poverty, inequality, or lack of access to education. A well-designed policy approach often requires a combination of nudging, regulation, and financial incentives to create lasting change. For example, while nudges can encourage people to use public transportation more frequently, substantial improvements in infrastructure and service reliability are necessary for long-term behavioral shifts.

In conclusion, Richard Thaler's nudge theory has revolutionized the way policymakers think about behavior change. By leveraging insights from psychology and behavioral economics, nudging offers a powerful tool for improving decision-making in areas such as health, finance, environmental conservation, and civic engagement. However, while nudges can be effective in guiding people toward better choices, they should be used ethically and in conjunction with broader policy measures. As technology and data analytics continue to evolve, the potential for behavioral policy tools will only grow, shaping the future of governance and public decision-making in profound ways.

Case Study: How Data Analytics Shaped Election Strategies

In the modern era of political campaigning, data analytics has transformed the way elections are fought and won. Gone are the days when political strategies relied solely on intuition, mass rallies, and broad messaging. Today, campaigns are driven by sophisticated data-driven insights that help parties and candidates target voters more precisely, craft persuasive messages, and optimize resource allocation. The use of big data, artificial intelligence, and predictive modeling has reshaped election strategies across the world, influencing everything from voter outreach to policy positioning.

One of the most famous cases of data-driven election strategy is Barack Obama's 2012 U.S. presidential campaign. While Obama's 2008 campaign had already revolutionized digital campaigning, the 2012 reelection bid took data analytics to an entirely new level. His team created a centralized database that merged voter records, social media interactions, and online engagement metrics to build highly detailed voter profiles. The campaign's analytics team, comprising data scientists, behavioral economists, and technology experts, used predictive modeling to assess which voters were most likely to be persuaded and what messages would resonate with them.

A key breakthrough was microtargeting, a strategy that involves segmenting voters into narrow demographic and behavioral categories and tailoring campaign messages specifically for them. Instead of broadcasting the same message to all voters, Obama's team used data-driven insights to send personalized emails, social media ads, and even door-to-door scripts. For example, suburban mothers received messages focused on healthcare and education, while young professionals were targeted with content about job creation and student debt relief. This level of precision significantly improved voter engagement and turnout among key demographics.

Another critical data-driven strategy involved A/B testing—a method commonly used in digital marketing to compare the effectiveness of different messages. The campaign tested various email subject lines, donation appeals, and social media ads to determine which versions performed best. A small change, such as using "Hey" instead of "Dear Supporter" in an email subject line, resulted in millions of dollars in additional donations. These insights allowed the campaign to optimize its communication strategy in real time, ensuring maximum impact.

Beyond digital communication, data analytics also played a crucial role in field operations. Volunteers knocking on doors were given smartphone apps with real-time voter data, guiding them to specific households that were most likely to be receptive. These apps not only provided information on voter preferences but also suggested conversation points based on previous interactions. This approach made door-to-door canvassing far more efficient, as campaigners were no longer wasting time on voters who were unlikely to change their minds.

While Obama's campaign demonstrated the power of data analytics in politics, Donald Trump's 2016 campaign showcased how social media-driven data strategies could be leveraged for highly targeted persuasion. A key player in Trump's digital operation was Cambridge Analytica, a controversial data analytics firm that used psychographic profiling to influence voter behavior. By harvesting vast amounts of Facebook user data, the company claimed to have developed psychological profiles of millions of American voters. These insights allowed Trump's team to create hyper-targeted political advertisements tailored to specific personality traits.

For instance, highly conservative voters were shown fear-based messaging about immigration and national security, while more moderate Republicans received messages focused on economic growth and tax cuts. Cambridge Analytica's methods were controversial and raised serious ethical concerns about voter manipulation and privacy breaches. Nevertheless, the 2016 election underscored how data analytics, when combined with psychological profiling, could be a game-changer in political campaigns.

India's elections have also witnessed a growing reliance on data-driven strategies. The Bharatiya Janata Party (BJP), under Prime Minister Narendra Modi, has been at the forefront of using data analytics to shape its electoral campaigns. In the 2014 and 2019 general elections, the BJP's campaign strategy was heavily influenced by big data analytics and social media engagement. The party utilized vast databases of voter demographics, social media activity, and historical voting patterns to fine-tune its messaging and mobilization efforts.

A major innovation was the NaMo App, a mobile application used to connect directly with millions of supporters. Through the app, Modi's campaign could send personalized messages, conduct opinion polls, and encourage grassroots activism. Additionally, the party's war rooms—high-tech command centers filled with data analysts—monitored social media trends in real time, allowing the campaign to adjust its messaging dynamically. If a particular issue was gaining traction online, the campaign quickly tailored its communication strategy to capitalize on it.

Furthermore, the BJP pioneered the use of WhatsApp groups for political mobilization. Since WhatsApp is one of the most widely used messaging platforms in India, the party created thousands of localized groups to disseminate campaign material, fact-check opposition claims, and coordinate ground-level activities. This decentralized approach, driven by data insights, helped the party reach voters in both urban and rural areas more effectively than traditional media.

Apart from election campaigns, data analytics is now being used by governments to shape public policy. In the U.K., the Vote Leave campaign during the Brexit referendum used targeted digital advertising based on voter data to influence undecided voters. Similarly, data-driven insights have been used to combat voter suppression, predict election fraud, and enhance civic engagement through apps and online platforms that provide real-time information on polling stations and voter registration.

However, the increasing reliance on data analytics in elections also raises ethical and legal concerns. The potential for misinformation, privacy violations, and algorithmic bias poses significant challenges. The misuse of data, as seen in the Cambridge Analytica scandal, highlights the need for stricter regulations on political data mining. Additionally, the rise of deepfake technology and AI-generated misinformation presents new threats to democratic processes. Governments and election commissions worldwide are now exploring ways to ensure transparency and accountability in data-driven campaigning.

In conclusion, data analytics has fundamentally reshaped election strategies, making campaigns more precise, efficient, and impactful. From Obama's data-driven voter outreach to Trump's psychographic targeting and Modi's WhatsApp mobilization, political campaigns are increasingly relying on technology to gain a competitive edge. While these innovations offer numerous advantages, they also come with ethical dilemmas that require careful oversight. As technology continues to evolve, the role of data in politics will only grow, influencing not just elections but governance itself. The challenge ahead lies in balancing innovation with ethical responsibility to ensure that democracy remains fair, transparent, and accessible to all.

CHAPTER NINE

Philosophy, Ethics, and Political Science – Rethinking Governance

Applying Ancient Political Thought to Modern Governance: Insights from Plato, Confucius, and Kautilya

Throughout history, some of the most profound thinkers have sought to understand power, governance, and justice. Their ideas, though developed in vastly different historical and cultural contexts, continue to influence modern political systems. Plato, the Greek philosopher, Confucius, the Chinese sage, and Kautilya, the Indian strategist, each contributed unique perspectives on governance, leadership, and ethics. Despite the centuries that separate them from today's world, their wisdom remains highly relevant, offering insights into leadership, policymaking, and institutional design.

Plato: The Philosopher-King and Just Governance

Plato, a disciple of Socrates, articulated his vision of an ideal state in The Republic. His most famous concept—the Philosopher-King—suggests that the best rulers should not be those who seek power for personal gain but those who possess wisdom, virtue, and philosophical insight. In Plato's ideal state, rulers undergo rigorous intellectual and moral training to ensure they prioritize the common good over personal interests.

This idea finds resonance in modern debates about political leadership and governance. Today, democratic systems emphasize electoral accountability, but the quality of leadership remains a concern. Plato's argument suggests that mere popularity or electoral success should not be the sole criteria for leadership; rather, a deep understanding of governance, ethics, and justice should be prioritized. While democracy values the voice of the people, Plato's insights encourage meritocratic elements in governance, such as expert-driven policymaking, independent institutions, and a well-educated civil service. Many modern governments, particularly technocratic regimes like Singapore, emphasize leadership grounded in expertise and rational decision-making, echoing Plato's call for rule by the most capable.

Another crucial element of Plato's thought is his idea of the Tripartite Soul, which parallels a well-balanced society. He argued that just as individuals have three components—reason, spirit, and desire—society also comprises three classes: rulers (wisdom), guardians (courage), and producers (economic needs). A well-functioning state, according to Plato, maintains harmony between these classes. Today, political stability and good governance rely on striking a balance between state institutions, security forces, and economic contributors. Over-dominance by any one sector—whether the military, corporate elites, or ideological movements—can destabilize the equilibrium, just as Plato warned.

Confucius: Moral Leadership and Ethical Governance

While Plato emphasized intellectual wisdom in governance, Confucius (551–479 BCE) focused on ethical leadership and virtue. His political philosophy, rooted in Confucianism, stresses the importance of rulers setting moral examples for their subjects. According to Confucius, a good leader should embody Ren (benevolence), Li (proper conduct), and Yi (righteousness). He argued that a virtuous ruler creates a virtuous society—if the government is corrupt, the people will follow its example.

This idea has strong implications for modern governance, particularly in combating corruption and promoting transparency. Many contemporary democracies face crises of trust in leadership due to scandals, nepotism, and unethical practices. Confucius's emphasis on moral integrity suggests that ethical leadership must be the foundation of any political system. Countries that emphasize strong moral leadership—such as those with strict anti-corruption measures—tend to have more stable and prosperous societies. The Scandinavian nations, for instance, have successfully integrated ethical governance into their political culture, ensuring trust between citizens and the state.

Confucius also introduced the concept of Meritocracy, arguing that government officials should be selected based on competence rather than birthright or wealth. This principle influenced the Chinese Imperial Examination system, which persisted for over a thousand years and still influences modern civil service exams in countries like China, India, and the United States. In today's world, ensuring that government officials are chosen based on merit rather than political favoritism aligns with Confucian ideals, strengthening public administration and governance effectiveness.

Moreover, Confucius's vision of social harmony through Filial Piety and Respect for Hierarchical Order provides insights into governance stability. While modern democracies emphasize individual rights, societies with Confucian traditions, such as Japan and South Korea, stress collective responsibility and respect for authority, contributing to disciplined governance and economic success. However, critics argue that excessive hierarchy can stifle innovation and suppress dissent, highlighting the need to balance Confucian respect for order with democratic pluralism.

Kautilya: Realpolitik and Strategic Governance

In contrast to Plato's idealism and Confucius's moralism, Kautilya (also known as Chanakya) offered a highly pragmatic and strategic approach to governance. Writing in Arthashastra (circa 4th century BCE), Kautilya provided a manual on statecraft, diplomacy, and economic management, akin to Machiavelli's The Prince but far more comprehensive. His philosophy was grounded in Realpolitik—the idea that rulers must act pragmatically rather than ideologically to maintain power and stability.

Kautilya's concept of governance was based on the idea that a strong and well-organized state was necessary for prosperity. He outlined the Saptanga Theory—seven essential elements of a state: the king, ministers, territory, fortifications, treasury, army, and allies. This model remains relevant in modern governance, where national strength is determined not only by political leadership but also by economic stability, security infrastructure, and diplomatic alliances.

One of Kautilya's most enduring lessons is his emphasis on Economic Governance. Unlike Plato and Confucius, who primarily focused on political and ethical dimensions, Kautilya saw economic stability as the foundation of good governance. He argued that a state must generate revenue through efficient taxation, trade policies, and wealth creation. Many of today's economic policies—such as progressive taxation, public infrastructure investment, and trade regulations—reflect Kautilya's insights into economic governance. Countries that prioritize long-term economic planning, such as Germany and China, exhibit principles found in Arthashastra, where economic strength ensures national security.

In diplomacy, Kautilya advocated the Mandala Theory, which describes a world of shifting alliances and rivalries. He argued that neighboring states are natural adversaries, while states further away can be potential allies. This concept is evident in contemporary geopolitics, where nations form strategic partnerships based on common interests rather than ideological alignment. India's current foreign policy, balancing ties with the U.S., Russia, and regional neighbors, mirrors Kautilya's emphasis on flexible and pragmatic diplomacy.

Additionally, Kautilya's thoughts on Espionage and Intelligence are strikingly modern. He advocated for a well-developed intelligence network to safeguard national security and prevent threats to the state. Today, intelligence agencies such as the CIA, MI6, and RAW function based on principles similar to Kautilya's ideas, where surveillance, information gathering, and strategic deception play crucial roles in national defense. His emphasis on internal security also finds relevance in counterterrorism efforts and cybersecurity strategies in modern governance.

Bridging Ancient Thought with Modern Governance

Despite their historical contexts, the ideas of Plato, Confucius, and Kautilya continue to offer valuable lessons for contemporary governance. Plato's focus on wisdom and justice highlights the need for capable and ethical leadership. Confucius's emphasis on virtue and meritocracy underscores the importance of moral governance and a competent civil service. Kautilya's pragmatic statecraft reveals the necessity of economic strength, strategic diplomacy, and intelligence in maintaining national stability.

Modern governance requires a synthesis of these ideas. While democratic systems prioritize popular participation, they must also integrate Plato's wisdom-based leadership, Confucius's ethical governance, and Kautilya's strategic statecraft. The key challenge for today's policymakers is to balance these ancient insights with contemporary democratic values, ensuring that governance remains just, effective, and adaptable to the complexities of the modern world. By revisiting these timeless philosophies, political leaders can create more resilient and forward-thinking governance structures that serve both the state and its people.

Ethical dilemmas in political decision-making

Ethical dilemmas in political decision-making are among the most complex challenges faced by leaders and policymakers. Every decision carries weight, affecting millions of lives, and often, there is no clear right or wrong choice—only difficult trade-offs. Political leaders are constantly forced to navigate between moral ideals and practical realities, balancing national interests with ethical principles. Whether it's deciding on military interventions, regulating surveillance, distributing wealth, or ensuring fair elections, the dilemmas are endless. These decisions are not made in isolation; they are shaped by history, public opinion, economic constraints, and global dynamics, making political ethics one of the most debated and scrutinized aspects of governance.

One of the most fundamental dilemmas is the tension between ethics and pragmatism. While leaders are expected to uphold justice and transparency, they must also ensure stability and progress. Take, for example, the question of negotiating with terrorist groups to secure the release of hostages. Ethically, many argue that engaging with terrorists legitimizes their actions and sets a dangerous precedent. However, from a practical standpoint, refusing to negotiate could result in innocent lives being lost. Similarly, during wartime, decisions about launching drone strikes against enemy combatants often weigh national security against the potential for civilian casualties. These choices force leaders to confront the grim reality that safeguarding one group may come at the cost of harming another.

Another persistent ethical dilemma is balancing individual rights with the collective good. This was particularly evident during the COVID-19 pandemic when governments had to choose between enforcing strict lockdowns to protect public health or allowing personal freedoms at the risk of spreading the virus. While lockdowns saved lives, they also led to severe economic disruptions, mental health crises, and restrictions on basic liberties. Similarly, mass surveillance programs are often justified in the name of national security, but they also raise concerns about privacy and government overreach. How much personal freedom should be sacrificed for safety? How do we ensure that such measures are not misused for political control? These are the kinds of questions policymakers must grapple with daily.

Economic policies present their own set of ethical challenges. Taxation, welfare programs, and government spending all involve difficult decisions about who should bear the financial burden of supporting society. Progressive taxation, where the wealthy pay higher rates, is often seen as a way to reduce income inequality. But opponents argue that heavy taxation discourages investment and innovation, ultimately harming economic growth. On the other hand, cutting taxes for corporations and the rich might stimulate business but can also widen the wealth gap, leaving millions without adequate access to healthcare, education, and other essential services. Striking a balance between economic efficiency and social justice is a never-ending struggle, with no universally accepted solution.

Foreign policy is another area riddled with ethical contradictions. Governments often have to choose between upholding human rights and maintaining strategic alliances. Consider the dilemma of selling arms to authoritarian regimes. Many powerful nations engage in arms sales, arguing that these transactions are essential for economic and geopolitical reasons. Yet, these same weapons are often used in conflicts that fuel human rights abuses. Similarly, military interventions intended to prevent genocide or civil war can end up destabilizing entire regions, as seen in Iraq and Libya. Should democratic nations engage with oppressive regimes in hopes of influencing gradual reform, or should they isolate them as a matter of principle? This is an ongoing ethical debate, with real-world consequences that impact millions.

Corruption in politics adds yet another layer to ethical dilemmas. While democratic systems are designed to prevent corruption, loopholes often allow unethical practices to thrive. Electoral manipulation, gerrymandering, and corporate lobbying blur the line between legal strategy and outright corruption. Politicians often justify such practices as necessary for political survival, arguing that the end justifies the means. But at what point does political strategy cross into moral failure? When does securing power become more important than serving the people? The erosion of public trust in government is often the result of these ethical failings, making it harder to implement policies that truly benefit society.

Climate change presents one of the greatest moral challenges of our time. Governments worldwide must decide how to balance economic development with environmental responsibility. Fossil fuel industries provide jobs and economic stability, but their long-term impact on the planet is devastating. Should leaders prioritize short-term economic gains or take bold action to combat climate change, even at the cost of industrial decline? International climate agreements like the Paris Accord require global cooperation, but ethical dilemmas emerge when developing countries argue that wealthier nations—who historically contributed more to climate change—should bear the greater burden. The debate over fairness, responsibility, and economic sustainability continues to shape global environmental policies.

Ethical decision-making in politics is never easy, and rarely does a single answer satisfy all perspectives. Leaders must constantly navigate the gray areas, where every choice carries both benefits and moral costs. The best solutions are often found not in rigid ideologies but in open dialogue, critical thinking, and a willingness to adapt to new realities. While ethical dilemmas will always be a part of governance, societies can move toward better decision-making by fostering transparency, public accountability, and ethical leadership. In the end, politics is not just about power and policy—it is about making choices that define the kind of world we want to live in.

Teaching students to navigate moral complexities in policy-making

Teaching students to navigate the moral complexities of policy-making is an essential aspect of preparing future leaders, analysts, and engaged citizens. In a world where governance decisions can have profound ethical consequences, it is crucial to equip students with the ability to critically evaluate policies not just on their effectiveness but also on their moral implications. Policy-making is rarely black and white—it involves trade-offs, competing interests, and ethical dilemmas that require deep thought and careful judgment. By integrating ethics into political education, students can develop the skills necessary to engage in thoughtful debate, make principled decisions, and understand the real-world impact of governance choices.

One of the most effective ways to teach students about moral complexities in policy-making is through case studies of historical and contemporary decisions. For example, examining the U.S. decision to drop atomic bombs on Hiroshima and Nagasaki allows students to grapple with the moral tension between ending a war swiftly and the devastating loss of civilian life. Similarly, analyzing government responses to pandemics, such as COVID-19, presents questions about the balance between public health and personal freedoms. Should governments enforce strict lockdowns to save lives at the cost of economic hardship? Or should they prioritize economic stability, knowing it may lead to higher mortality rates? Engaging with such cases forces students to think beyond simplistic answers and recognize the layered nature of policy decisions.

Debates and structured discussions also play a key role in helping students understand ethical complexities. By participating in Socratic seminars, mock legislative debates, or Model UN sessions, students are encouraged to view issues from multiple perspectives. They may be assigned roles that do not align with their personal beliefs, challenging them to develop arguments based on logic, precedent, and ethical reasoning rather than personal bias. For instance, debating the morality of capital punishment, affirmative action, or refugee policies helps students explore questions of justice, fairness, and human rights in a structured way. These exercises teach them that in real-world policy-making, leaders often have to make decisions that satisfy neither extreme but instead aim for the most justifiable compromise.

Another crucial element in ethical education is helping students understand the role of unintended consequences in policy-making. Many policies, though well-intended, can produce negative side effects. For example, the "War on Drugs" in the United States was launched with the goal of reducing drug abuse but led to mass incarceration, disproportionately affecting marginalized communities. Similarly, policies like universal basic income, which aim to reduce poverty, raise ethical questions about economic dependency and the responsibility of individuals versus the state. Teaching students to anticipate and evaluate unintended consequences fosters a more nuanced approach to policy analysis, ensuring they recognize that even the most ethically sound decisions can lead to complex outcomes.

Incorporating role-playing and simulations into political science education can further deepen students' understanding of ethical dilemmas in policy-making. UN simulations, crisis decision-making exercises, or national security war games immerse students in high-pressure situations where they must make choices with moral and political consequences. For instance, a simulation in which students must decide how to allocate limited medical supplies during a humanitarian crisis forces them to confront difficult ethical questions. Who should receive aid first—children, the elderly, or frontline workers? These exercises build empathy, critical thinking, and decision-making skills by placing students in the position of real-world policymakers.

Teaching media literacy is another essential aspect of ethical education in policy-making. In today's digital age, misinformation, political propaganda, and bias in media reporting can shape public perception of policies in misleading ways. Students must learn to critically assess news sources, distinguish between fact and opinion, and identify how framing and language influence policy debates. For example, the way immigration policies are reported—whether framed as a humanitarian issue or a national security threat—can shape public support and political action. Equipping students with these analytical skills ensures that they engage with policy debates as informed citizens rather than passive consumers of information.

Moreover, introducing students to different ethical frameworks—such as utilitarianism, deontology, and virtue ethics—can help them develop a structured approach to evaluating policies. Utilitarianism, which prioritizes the greatest good for the greatest number, can justify policies like vaccine mandates or progressive taxation. Deontological ethics, which emphasize duty and principles, might argue against any form of surveillance that infringes on personal privacy, regardless of its benefits. Virtue ethics, which focus on moral character, may encourage leaders to act with integrity and compassion even in politically difficult situations. Teaching students these frameworks allows them to analyze policies with a deeper understanding of the moral reasoning behind them.

Ultimately, preparing students to navigate the moral complexities of policy-making is about cultivating ethical leadership and informed decision-making. In an era of rapid technological advancements, global crises, and increasing political polarization, the ability to think critically about ethical dilemmas is more crucial than ever. By integrating ethics into political science education, educators can empower students to approach policy debates with empathy, logic, and a commitment to justice. Whether they become policymakers, activists, or engaged citizens, students trained in ethical reasoning will be better equipped to contribute to a fairer and more just society.

Career Readiness and Future Pathways

CHAPTER TEN

Skill Development for Political Science Students

Policy Writing, Advocacy, and Research Methodology

Effective policy writing, advocacy, and research methodology are crucial skills for anyone interested in shaping public policy, influencing governance, or driving social change. Policy-making is not just about having good ideas—it requires structured research, persuasive advocacy, and clear, evidence-based writing. Whether working in government, think tanks, NGOs, or international organizations, individuals engaged in policy work must learn how to craft compelling policy documents, conduct rigorous research, and effectively communicate their recommendations to decision-makers.

At the heart of policy writing lies the ability to present complex issues in a clear, concise, and actionable manner. Policy documents such as white papers, policy briefs, and legislative proposals must be structured logically, presenting the problem, evidence, and recommendations in a way that is accessible to policymakers. A well-written policy document typically begins with an executive summary, outlining the issue and the proposed solution in a few paragraphs. This is followed by a background section that provides context, historical developments, and key stakeholders. Next, the analysis section delves into data, research findings, and potential policy options. Finally, the recommendation section presents a well-argued, feasible, and evidence-backed course of action. Writing in a clear, jargon-free language is essential because policymakers often have limited time and must be able to grasp the core argument quickly.

Advocacy plays a critical role in ensuring that well-researched policies gain traction and are implemented effectively. Advocacy is the process of influencing public opinion, government officials, and institutions to adopt certain policies or reforms. Effective advocacy combines storytelling with empirical evidence to create a persuasive narrative. Activists, lobbyists, and policy professionals often engage in various forms of advocacy, such as grassroots mobilization, media campaigns, and direct lobbying of government officials. Social media has also emerged as a powerful tool for advocacy, allowing individuals and organizations to reach large audiences, engage in digital activism, and apply pressure on policymakers through viral campaigns. However, advocacy is not just about passion; it requires strategic planning, coalition-building, and the ability to frame issues in a way that resonates with different stakeholders.

A key component of both policy writing and advocacy is solid research methodology. Without rigorous research, policy proposals risk being ineffective, unrealistic, or even harmful. Research in policy-making involves both qualitative and quantitative methods, depending on the nature of the issue being addressed. Quantitative research relies on statistical data, surveys, and economic modeling to identify trends, correlations, and potential policy outcomes. For example, analyzing crime statistics can help shape better policing policies, while economic data can inform tax reforms. On the other hand, qualitative research involves interviews, case studies, and ethnographic analysis to understand the lived experiences of people affected by a policy. For instance, gathering testimonies from marginalized communities can shed light on the unintended consequences of certain welfare programs.

One of the most important aspects of research in policy-making is ensuring credibility and avoiding bias. Policymakers and stakeholders rely on research to make informed decisions, so the methods used must be transparent, replicable, and free from political or ideological influence. Peer-reviewed academic journals, government reports, and data from reputable institutions like the United Nations, World Bank, or national statistical agencies are valuable sources of information. Additionally, think tanks and research organizations contribute by publishing in-depth policy studies, though it is important to consider their ideological leanings when evaluating their findings.

Teaching students and professionals how to conduct policy research involves introducing them to various methodologies, including policy analysis frameworks such as cost-benefit analysis, stakeholder analysis, and impact assessment. Cost-benefit analysis helps determine whether the financial and social benefits of a policy outweigh its costs, making it a useful tool for deciding on budgetary allocations. Stakeholder analysis identifies the groups and individuals who will be affected by a policy and assesses their interests and influence. Impact assessment evaluates the potential long-term consequences of a policy, helping to anticipate unintended side effects and avoid policy failures.

One emerging trend in policy research and advocacy is the use of technology to enhance data collection and communication. Artificial intelligence, big data analytics, and digital platforms have revolutionized how policies are researched and promoted. For instance, AI can analyze vast amounts of public data to identify policy gaps and predict future trends. Social media analytics can track public sentiment on key issues, helping policymakers gauge public opinion in real time. Geographic Information Systems (GIS) mapping can visualize policy impact, such as tracking environmental degradation or mapping poverty levels across regions. These technological tools are increasingly shaping modern policy-making by providing real-time, data-driven insights that traditional research methods often lack.

Despite the increasing reliance on data and digital tools, ethical considerations remain central to policy writing, advocacy, and research. Policies must be crafted with an awareness of social justice, human rights, and the potential unintended consequences of government actions. Ethical research practices demand honesty in reporting findings, transparency in methodology, and a commitment to protecting the privacy and dignity of individuals involved in research studies. Advocacy, too, must be conducted with integrity, ensuring that campaigns are based on truthful information rather than manipulation or misinformation.

Ultimately, policy writing, advocacy, and research methodology are interconnected skills that empower individuals to drive meaningful change. Whether influencing government legislation, designing social programs, or advocating for underrepresented communities, those engaged in policy work must be equipped with the ability to conduct thorough research, craft persuasive arguments, and strategically promote their ideas. By mastering these skills, students, activists, and professionals can contribute to more effective, equitable, and evidence-based policy-making, shaping societies for the better.

Quantitative vs. Qualitative Research in Political Science

Research in political science relies on two primary approaches: quantitative and qualitative research. Each method provides unique insights into political behavior, institutions, and policies, and understanding their differences is crucial for scholars, policymakers, and analysts. While quantitative research focuses on numerical data, patterns, and statistical analysis, qualitative research delves into in-depth narratives, historical accounts, and subjective interpretations. Both approaches complement each other, offering a comprehensive understanding of political phenomena.

Quantitative research in political science employs numerical data to analyze trends, correlations, and causal relationships. This method often involves large datasets, surveys, experiments, and statistical modeling to draw objective conclusions about political behavior. For example, election studies use polling data to predict voting patterns and analyze the impact of demographic factors on electoral outcomes. Political scientists also apply regression analysis to study the correlation between economic growth and political stability, or they may use machine learning algorithms to detect trends in political speeches and media coverage. By using empirical evidence, quantitative research provides measurable and replicable findings, making it a valuable tool for policy-making and governance.

One of the biggest advantages of quantitative research is its ability to identify broad patterns across large populations. Consider the study of public opinion—surveys conducted across different regions can reveal national sentiment on key issues like economic policies, foreign relations, or governance. Similarly, political scientists use statistical techniques such as time-series analysis to assess how public policies affect economic performance over time. However, while quantitative research provides generalizable findings, it often struggles to capture the depth and complexity of political decision-making. Numbers can indicate trends, but they may not explain the motivations, emotions, or cultural contexts behind those trends.

On the other hand, qualitative research in political science is centered around detailed, contextual, and interpretive analysis. It involves case studies, interviews, historical research, ethnography, and content analysis to explore the deeper meaning of political events and behaviors. Unlike quantitative methods, which prioritize numerical objectivity, qualitative research emphasizes understanding the subjective experiences of political actors. For instance, an ethnographic study of political protests can provide rich insights into the motivations, emotions, and ideological beliefs of participants. Similarly, analyzing speeches, debates, or policy documents through discourse analysis allows researchers to understand the rhetoric and framing strategies used by politicians.

Qualitative research is particularly useful in studying complex political phenomena that cannot be easily quantified. For example, a researcher examining authoritarian regimes may conduct in-depth interviews with political dissidents to understand the psychological and strategic dimensions of political resistance. Similarly, a case study on conflict resolution in post-civil war societies may uncover how historical grievances, cultural traditions, and informal power structures shape peace negotiations. These aspects may not be adequately captured through surveys or statistical models, highlighting the necessity of qualitative methods.

One of the main criticisms of qualitative research is its potential for subjectivity and limited generalizability. Since qualitative studies often focus on specific cases, their findings may not be universally applicable. Additionally, researchers' interpretations may be influenced by personal biases or ideological perspectives. However, the depth of understanding provided by qualitative research is invaluable for exploring political narratives, ideological developments, and the lived experiences of individuals within political systems.

The debate between quantitative and qualitative research in political science is not about which method is superior but rather how they can complement each other. Mixed-methods research, which combines both approaches, is increasingly popular among political scientists. For example, a study on voter behavior might use surveys (quantitative) to collect large-scale data on voting patterns while also conducting interviews (qualitative) to understand the emotional and cultural reasons behind voters' choices. Similarly, an analysis of international relations may use statistical models to examine trade patterns while incorporating historical case studies to contextualize diplomatic decisions.

Ultimately, both quantitative and qualitative research play essential roles in political science. Quantitative methods provide objective, large-scale insights into political trends, while qualitative methods offer deeper, contextualized understandings of political behavior and institutions. By integrating both approaches, political scientists can develop more comprehensive and nuanced analyses, leading to better policy recommendations and a richer understanding of political life.

Writing Op-eds, Policy Briefs & Research Papers

Writing op-eds, policy briefs, and research papers is an essential skill for political scientists, policymakers, and public intellectuals. These forms of writing allow scholars and analysts to communicate their ideas effectively to different audiences, from policymakers and media professionals to the general public. While each format serves a unique purpose, they all require clear argumentation, persuasive reasoning, and a strong understanding of the subject matter.

Op-eds, or opinion editorials, are short, persuasive articles published in newspapers, magazines, or online platforms. They are designed to influence public opinion and decision-makers by presenting a well-reasoned argument on a current political or social issue. Op-eds typically range from 600 to 800 words and must be engaging, accessible, and backed by evidence. A strong op-ed starts with a compelling hook—perhaps a striking statistic, a personal anecdote, or a recent event—to grab the reader's attention. The body of the op-ed builds the argument logically, using facts, examples, and expert opinions. The conclusion offers a clear takeaway or a call to action, urging readers to consider a new perspective or support a policy change. For example, an op-ed on climate policy might begin with the increasing frequency of extreme weather events, discuss the economic and environmental impact of inaction, and conclude by advocating for stronger governmental regulations or international cooperation.

Unlike op-eds, policy briefs are targeted at decision-makers and policymakers who need concise, evidence-based insights to guide their actions. A policy brief is typically 2-4 pages long and provides a clear overview of an issue, supported by data, research findings, and policy recommendations. The structure of a policy brief includes an executive summary, background information, an analysis of the problem, potential solutions, and specific recommendations. Clarity and brevity are essential since policymakers often have limited time to engage with lengthy documents. For example, a policy brief on education reform might present statistics on declining literacy rates, analyze the causes (such as lack of teacher training or outdated curricula), and propose solutions like increased investment in teacher development or curriculum modernization. Effective policy briefs rely on compelling visuals, such as graphs or infographics, to present complex data in an easily digestible format.

In contrast, research papers are in-depth, scholarly documents that contribute to academic discourse and provide rigorous analysis of political issues. Research papers typically follow a structured format, including an abstract, introduction, literature review, methodology, data analysis, discussion, and conclusion. Unlike op-eds and policy briefs, which are designed for immediate impact, research papers undergo extensive peer review and contribute to long-term knowledge building. A well-crafted research paper begins with a clear research question, explores existing literature on the topic, and employs either qualitative or quantitative methods to analyze data. For instance, a research paper on voter suppression might examine historical case studies, analyze voting data, and use statistical models to assess the impact of specific policies. The findings are then discussed in the context of broader political theories, offering both empirical evidence and theoretical insights.

Each of these writing formats plays a crucial role in shaping political discourse. Op-eds serve as tools for advocacy, engaging the public and generating debate. Policy briefs provide actionable recommendations for decision-makers, influencing legislative and executive decisions. Research papers contribute to academic knowledge, providing a foundation for future studies and policy innovations. While these formats differ in style, length, and audience, they all require critical thinking, strong argumentation, and clear communication.

Mastering these writing styles enhances one's ability to participate in political debates, contribute to policy discussions, and advance scholarly research. Whether addressing the public through a newspaper, advising policymakers through a brief, or contributing to academia through rigorous research, the ability to write effectively is a powerful tool in shaping political and social change.

CHAPTER ELEVEN

The Future of Political Science Careers & Education

How political science education must adapt for future careers

Political science education must evolve to meet the demands of an increasingly complex, digital, and interconnected world. The traditional focus on political theory, governance structures, and historical analysis remains essential, but future careers in the field require a broader, more interdisciplinary approach. Graduates must be equipped with practical skills, technological literacy, and global awareness to navigate new political, economic, and social challenges. To stay relevant, political science education must integrate data analytics, digital tools, policy-making simulations, and experiential learning opportunities that align with emerging career paths.

One of the most significant shifts in political science education must be the integration of technology and data analytics. Modern politics is heavily influenced by big data, artificial intelligence, and digital platforms. From election forecasting and policy modeling to real-time public opinion tracking, political scientists today must understand how to interpret and leverage data. Universities should incorporate courses on quantitative methods, Python for data analysis, R for statistical modeling, and GIS mapping to prepare students for data-driven decision-making roles in government, think tanks, and political consulting firms.

Another crucial area of transformation is the rise of digital diplomacy and cyber governance. International relations are no longer confined to diplomatic meetings and treaties; much of global politics now unfolds on digital platforms. Social media diplomacy ("Twiplomacy"), cyber warfare, and digital activism have changed how states and non-state actors engage with each other. Political science curricula should include courses on cybersecurity, misinformation analysis, digital communication strategies, and ethical considerations in AI governance. Understanding how global powers use digital tools for influence—whether through social media campaigns, cyberattacks, or blockchain-based governance models—is crucial for the next generation of political leaders and analysts.

Experiential learning and real-world applications must become central to political science education. Traditional classroom-based learning should be supplemented with hands-on experiences such as Model United Nations (MUN), Model Parliament, mock court trials, and crisis simulations. These interactive methods prepare students for high-pressure decision-making environments in government agencies, NGOs, and international organizations. Case studies on real-world political events, such as election campaigns, international negotiations, and policy failures, should be incorporated into coursework to provide students with practical insights.

Moreover, interdisciplinary learning is essential for future political scientists. The field increasingly overlaps with economics, psychology, environmental studies, and business administration. Courses on behavioral economics, public policy design, climate politics, and international trade regulations should be integrated into political science programs. This broader approach ensures that graduates can work across sectors, whether in global governance, corporate social responsibility, or political risk analysis.

Political science education must also emphasize skills in policy writing, advocacy, and public communication. The ability to write compelling policy briefs, craft persuasive op-eds, and analyze legislative proposals is crucial for careers in public policy and governance. Students should be trained in media literacy, public speaking, and digital storytelling to effectively communicate political ideas in an age dominated by visual and digital media.

Political science programs must prepare students for non-traditional careers beyond government and academia. The private sector increasingly seeks political science graduates for roles in corporate lobbying, political consulting, artificial intelligence ethics, and sustainability governance.

Universities should offer career counseling and internship opportunities that expose students to roles in technology firms, financial institutions, and international development agencies.

Political science education must move beyond traditional theory-based approaches and embrace a dynamic, skills-based curriculum that prepares students for the future. By integrating technology, experiential learning, interdisciplinary studies, and communication training, political science programs can equip students with the tools they need to navigate the evolving political landscape and thrive in a wide range of careers.

Entrepreneurship in Political Science (Ed-Tech, Consulting, Media Analysis)

Entrepreneurship in political science is an emerging and exciting avenue that blends political expertise with innovation, business acumen, and technology. Traditionally, political science graduates have pursued careers in government, academia, or policy research. However, the rise of Ed-Tech platforms, consulting firms, and media analysis ventures has opened up new entrepreneurial opportunities. These avenues allow political scientists to shape public discourse, provide expert insights, and create sustainable businesses that influence governance, education, and policymaking.

One of the most promising areas of political science entrepreneurship is Ed-Tech (Educational Technology). With the increasing demand for online learning and specialized knowledge, political science educators and researchers can create digital learning platforms, online courses, and skill-based training programs. Platforms like Coursera, edX, and Swayam have already demonstrated the success of online political education, but there remains a vast market for customized courses on policy analysis, global governance, electoral politics, and political theory. Entrepreneurs can develop subscription-based learning portals, interactive e-learning modules, or AI-driven personalized tutoring services to cater to students, civil service aspirants, and professionals.

Another major entrepreneurial path is political consulting and advisory services. In an era where data analytics, behavioral insights, and strategic communication shape electoral outcomes, political science professionals can establish consulting firms specializing in campaign strategy, opinion polling, public relations, and governance advisory. Many political leaders, corporate entities, and NGOs seek data-driven decision-making support, voter sentiment analysis, and political risk assessments to navigate the complex political landscape. By leveraging AI-driven predictive modeling, GIS-based electoral mapping, and behavioral psychology insights, entrepreneurs can offer high-value services that enhance election campaigns, policy decisions, and public engagement strategies.

The media analysis sector is another lucrative space for political entrepreneurs. With the explosion of digital media, social media diplomacy, and AI-driven news dissemination, political scientists can establish fact-checking platforms, media watchdog organizations, and analytical news portals. Misinformation and propaganda have become significant global concerns, and there is a growing demand for unbiased, research-backed political analysis. By utilizing natural language processing (NLP) tools, AI-driven sentiment analysis, and digital storytelling techniques, entrepreneurs can create news platforms, YouTube channels, or podcasts that break down complex political events in an engaging and accessible way.

Beyond these core areas, there is immense potential for entrepreneurship in public affairs, advocacy, and civic engagement platforms. Startups can focus on civic tech solutions, such as digital voting awareness campaigns, legislative tracking apps, or AI-powered policy recommendation tools. Nonprofits and businesses alike require experts who can bridge the gap between government policies and public needs, making this a valuable space for politically informed entrepreneurs.

Entrepreneurship in political science requires a mix of academic expertise, technological fluency, and business strategy. By combining political insights with innovation in Ed-Tech, consulting, and media, political scientists can create impactful ventures that not only shape public understanding but also drive meaningful change in governance, democracy, and policymaking. As technology continues to evolve, the intersection of political knowledge and entrepreneurship will become even more critical, offering immense potential for growth and influence.

Internship and Fellowship Opportunities for Political Science Students

Internships and fellowships are crucial stepping stones for political science students, offering hands-on experience, professional networking, and a deeper understanding of real-world political dynamics. Unlike traditional classroom learning, internships and fellowships provide immersive exposure to governance, policy-making, international relations, and political analysis. They serve as a bridge between academic theories and practical applications, shaping students into future policymakers, analysts, diplomats, and thought leaders.

One of the most sought-after avenues is government and legislative internships, where students work directly with elected officials, government departments, or public policy bodies. Opportunities such as internships with Members of Parliament, state legislatures, or ministries allow students to engage in policy research, draft legislative briefs, and participate in governance discussions. Programs like the LAMP Fellowship (Legislative Assistants to Members of Parliament) in India or the White House Internship Program in the U.S. provide unparalleled exposure to lawmaking and political processes. These experiences help students develop analytical skills, understand legislative structures, and contribute to policy formulation.

For those interested in international relations and diplomacy, internships with organizations like the United Nations (UN), Ministry of External Affairs, embassies, and international think tanks offer firsthand experience in global governance. Programs such as the UN Young Professionals Programme (YPP), internships at the World Bank, or research assistantships at the Observer Research Foundation (ORF) allow students to engage in international policy discussions, geopolitical analysis, and global problem-solving. These opportunities are particularly valuable for those aiming for careers in foreign service, international organizations, or diplomatic advisory roles.

Another critical area is public policy and research-based fellowships, where students work with think tanks, advocacy groups, and research institutions. Fellowships such as the RBI Young Scholars Program, Carnegie India Research Fellowship, or the Brookings Institution Internship help students dive deep into data-driven policymaking, governance strategies, and economic-political linkages. These roles involve conducting policy research, drafting white papers, and engaging with policymakers to propose innovative solutions to pressing societal challenges.

The media and political communication sector also offers extensive opportunities for political science students. Interning with news agencies, digital media platforms, or political consulting firms provides training in political journalism, campaign strategy, and public relations. Programs with organizations like The Print, The Hindu Centre for Politics and Public

Policy, or the BBC Political Journalism Internship equip students with skills in political reporting, media analysis, and strategic communication—critical for careers in political commentary, electoral strategy, and advocacy.

For students passionate about grassroots politics and activism, internships with NGOs, human rights organizations, and civic engagement groups can be transformative. Programs like Teach for India Fellowship, PRS Legislative Research Internship, or internships at Amnesty International provide hands-on experience in community development, governance accountability, and human rights advocacy. These roles help students understand the intersection of politics and social justice while allowing them to work closely with marginalized communities.

Many corporate and financial organizations also offer fellowships focusing on political risk analysis, regulatory affairs, and economic policy, which are growing fields in political science careers. Internships with global risk advisory firms, consulting giants like McKinsey and PwC, or economic policy divisions in financial institutions provide insights into how businesses navigate government policies and international regulations.

To make the most of these opportunities, students should actively apply for structured internship programs, attend political conferences, engage in networking events, and participate in research projects. By gaining exposure to real-world political challenges and policy implementation, students can develop expertise in governance, diplomacy, and advocacy—paving the way for impactful careers in the political landscape.

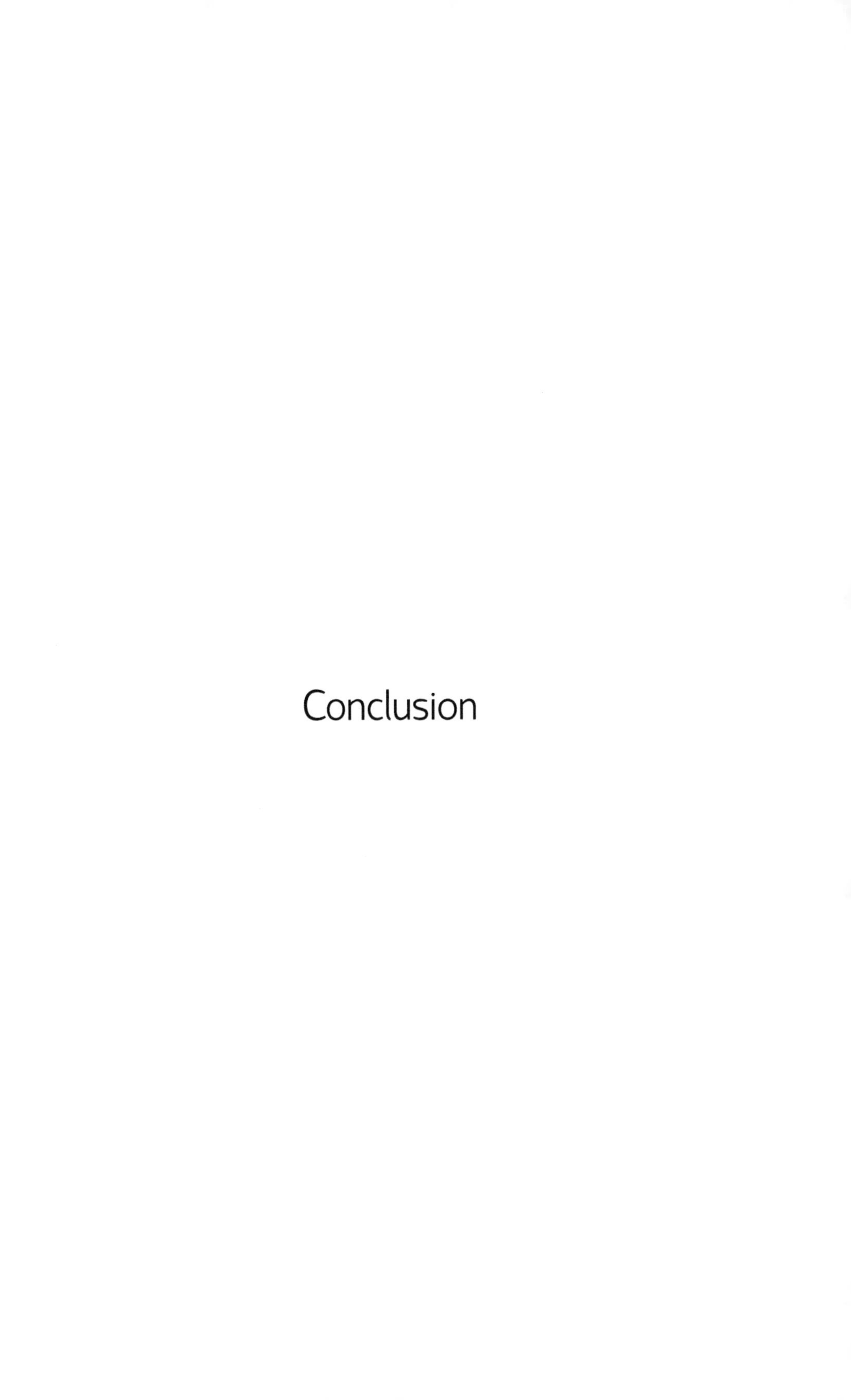

Conclusion

CHAPTER TWELVE

The Road Ahead for Political Science Education

How educators and students can adapt to the new paradigm

The world of political science education is rapidly evolving, influenced by technological advancements, new learning methodologies, and the changing demands of the workforce. Educators and students must embrace these shifts to remain relevant and make the most of the opportunities available in the digital age. The traditional classroom, with its heavy reliance on textbooks and rote learning, is being replaced by interactive, technology-driven, and skill-based approaches that emphasize critical thinking, practical application, and interdisciplinary learning.

For educators, adapting to this new paradigm requires a shift from being mere transmitters of information to becoming facilitators of knowledge and skill development. One of the most significant changes is the integration of technology-enhanced learning. Platforms like MOOCs (Massive Open Online Courses), AI-driven tutoring systems, and gamified learning tools provide opportunities for personalized learning experiences. Professors must explore blended learning methods, where in-person instruction is complemented by digital resources such as online simulations, discussion forums, and AI-generated assessments. This approach allows students to engage with material at their own pace, reinforcing concepts through interactive experiences rather than passive lectures.

Another major shift is the emphasis on experiential learning, where students engage in role-playing activities, debates, and real-world problem-solving exercises. For example, incorporating Model UN simulations, mock legislative debates, or policy-writing workshops enables students to apply political theories to contemporary issues, preparing them for careers in governance, diplomacy, and advocacy. Educators must design curricula that focus not just on theoretical knowledge but also on practical application through case studies, simulations, and collaborative projects that mirror real-life political challenges.

For students, adapting to this changing landscape means developing a proactive, self-driven approach to learning. No longer can they rely solely on classroom instruction; instead, they must seek out internships, fellowships, and digital learning resources to supplement their education. Platforms like Coursera, edX, and Swayam offer courses on policy analysis, data-driven governance, and political risk assessment, which can be valuable additions to a traditional political science degree. AI-powered research tools, online political forums, and digital archives enable students to conduct independent research, track policy developments, and engage in global discussions.

One of the most critical skills in this new paradigm is data literacy. With the increasing role of big data, artificial intelligence, and predictive analytics in politics, students must develop proficiency in data analysis, visualization, and digital research methodologies. Learning tools such as Python for political data analysis, R for statistical modeling, and GIS for political mapping can give students an edge in careers related to policy consulting, electoral strategy, and international relations research.

Another essential aspect of adaptation is developing strong critical thinking and media literacy skills. In an age of fake news, deepfakes, and AI-generated misinformation, both educators and students must become adept at analyzing sources, verifying facts, and understanding the role of algorithms in shaping public opinion. Courses on digital media analysis, propaganda studies, and information warfare should be integrated into the political science curriculum to equip students with the tools to navigate and combat misinformation in politics.

Collaboration is also key to succeeding in this new environment. Educators must foster multidisciplinary approaches, encouraging students to explore intersections between political science and fields like economics, technology, psychology, and environmental studies. Real-world political problems are complex and require solutions that draw from multiple disciplines. Students, in turn, should engage in team-based projects, cross-disciplinary research, and global discussions to broaden their perspectives and develop problem-solving skills relevant to today's interconnected world.

Adapting to this new paradigm requires a shift in mindset—one that values lifelong learning, adaptability, and resilience. Political landscapes are constantly evolving, and the ability to continuously learn, unlearn, and relearn will define the success of both educators and students. By embracing technology, enhancing analytical skills, and engaging in experiential learning, political science education can become more dynamic, relevant, and impactful in shaping the leaders, policymakers, and analysts of tomorrow.

Creating a globally relevant, interdisciplinary political science curriculum

Creating a globally relevant, interdisciplinary political science curriculum requires a departure from traditional nation-centric approaches and a move towards holistic, interconnected, and skill-based learning. Political science today is not just about studying governments and ideologies—it's about understanding how global trends, economic forces, technological advancements, and historical contexts shape political systems. To prepare students for careers in diplomacy, governance, international relations, policy analysis, and global consultancy, curricula must be designed with an interdisciplinary and practical approach.

One of the key shifts required is expanding the scope of political science beyond Western political thought and governance models. While thinkers like Plato, Locke, and Machiavelli remain essential, it is equally important to introduce Confucian philosophy, Kautilya's Arthashastra, Ibn Khaldun's sociopolitical theories, and African indigenous governance structures. By doing so, students gain a more comprehensive understanding of how different civilizations have conceptualized power, governance, and statecraft.

A globally relevant curriculum must also emphasize comparative politics and transnational issues. Rather than focusing solely on national governance models, students should explore regional organizations (EU, ASEAN, AU, SAARC), international institutions (UN, WTO, ICC), and global political movements (decolonization, climate change activism, human rights advocacy). Courses should examine how policies are shaped by global agreements such as the Paris Climate Accord, Universal

Declaration of Human Rights, and international trade regulations, helping students connect national policies to broader global trends.

The interdisciplinary nature of political science must be fully embraced. Economics, technology, psychology, law, and environmental studies all play an essential role in shaping modern political discourse. A well-rounded curriculum should include courses on behavioral economics in policymaking (Nudge Theory), political psychology (voter behavior, propaganda analysis), AI and big data in governance, and environmental politics (sustainability policies, climate diplomacy). The world is moving towards data-driven governance, making it crucial for students to gain exposure to quantitative analysis, policy modeling, and digital tools such as GIS mapping for political geography, Python for data analysis, and AI-based public sentiment tracking.

Practical application and skill-building must be at the core of political science education. Traditional essay-based assessments should be supplemented with policy writing exercises, real-world case studies, crisis simulations, and policy advocacy projects. Courses should encourage students to draft policy briefs, conduct mock parliamentary sessions, engage in United Nations simulations, and participate in debates on pressing international issues. Exposure to internships, fellowships, and real-world political consulting projects should be an integral part of academic programs, allowing students to transition seamlessly from theoretical learning to professional application.

Given the rapid digital transformation in politics, students must also develop skills in media literacy, cybersecurity awareness, and digital diplomacy. Political strategies today are shaped by social media campaigns, algorithm-driven propaganda, and misinformation warfare. A curriculum designed for the modern world must include training on detecting misinformation, analyzing digital narratives, and understanding the role of AI in political decision-making. The rise of Twiplomacy (Twitter Diplomacy), blockchain in governance, and cyber warfare means that political science students must be prepared for challenges that did not exist even a decade ago.

Another crucial component is fostering cross-cultural and multilingual competencies. A political science graduate in today's world is expected to navigate international negotiations, multicultural workplaces, and cross-border policy frameworks. Therefore, programs should integrate language training, global exchange programs, and partnerships with foreign universities to expose students to diverse political landscapes. Collaborative research projects with institutions from different continents can further deepen understanding of international politics and governance models.

Finally, a globally relevant curriculum must place an emphasis on ethics, leadership, and civic engagement. As students prepare for careers that influence governance, policymaking, and international relations, they must develop a strong ethical foundation. Courses should encourage critical discussions on political corruption, ethical dilemmas in policymaking, power dynamics in global institutions, and the responsibilities of public officials.

By integrating interdisciplinary knowledge, global perspectives, digital competencies, real-world applications, and ethical leadership, a political science curriculum can be transformed into a powerful tool for preparing the next generation of political leaders, analysts, and policymakers. The world is changing rapidly, and political science education must evolve to meet these new demands, ensuring that students are equipped to navigate, analyze, and shape the political landscape of the future.

Final reflections and recommendations

The field of political science is undergoing a profound transformation, shaped by technological advancements, global interconnectedness, and evolving political landscapes. As the discipline expands beyond traditional frameworks, it must equip students, educators, and policymakers with the skills and knowledge necessary to navigate modern governance, international relations, and digital-age politics. This book has explored innovative approaches to political science education, from flipped classrooms and AI-driven learning to policy simulations and behavioral insights, all aimed at fostering critical thinking, adaptability, and real-world application.

One of the most important takeaways from this discussion is the need for an interdisciplinary and globally relevant approach. The days of political science being a purely theoretical field, confined to textbooks and historical analyses, are long gone. Today, it is deeply intertwined with economics, technology, psychology, media, and environmental studies. Future curricula must embrace these intersections, ensuring that students are prepared for the complexity of policymaking, governance, and global diplomacy. This means breaking away from rigid academic boundaries and allowing students to engage with subjects in a way that mirrors the real-world challenges they will face.

Another crucial insight is the value of experiential learning. Theoretical knowledge alone is insufficient in a world where political decisions have immediate and far-reaching consequences. Model United Nations conferences, parliamentary simulations, policy labs, and crisis decision-making exercises provide students with hands-on experiences that bridge the gap between theory and practice. These approaches not only enhance their problem-solving abilities, negotiation skills, and leadership qualities but also prepare them for roles in government, international organizations, and think tanks. The ability to think critically under pressure, anticipate consequences, and adapt strategies in real time is essential for future leaders and policymakers.

Technology and data have also become indispensable to political science. AI-driven policy analysis, election forecasting, blockchain-based governance, and digital diplomacy are not just futuristic concepts but present realities that are reshaping how politics functions. Political science programs must integrate data literacy, coding for policy research, cybersecurity awareness, and misinformation detection to ensure that students can interpret trends, make informed decisions, and combat digital manipulation. Without these skills, political analysts and policymakers risk being left behind in an era where data-driven decision-making is the foundation of governance.

At the same time, ethical considerations in political science have never been more relevant. The challenges of propaganda, fake news, cyber warfare, and political corruption demand that future leaders and analysts be trained in ethical decision-making, civic responsibility, and the moral dilemmas of governance. If political science fails to address these concerns, it risks producing individuals who understand the mechanisms of power but lack the moral compass to use them responsibly. Educators must cultivate a sense of integrity, social responsibility, and accountability in students to prevent power from being wielded irresponsibly.

To address these challenges, universities and institutions must update political science programs to include AI, big data, behavioral science, and cybersecurity in governance. Courses on digital diplomacy, cyber warfare, and misinformation analysis should become standard. Encouraging interdisciplinary learning by combining political science with economics, law, environmental studies, and technology will help build a well-rounded understanding of global issues. Additionally, hands-on simulations, role-playing exercises, and real-world policy projects should be a core component of political science education to ensure that students are not just observers of politics but active participants.

Moreover, students must be trained in using modern analytical tools such as Python, R, GIS mapping, and AI-driven analytics to work with real-time political data. Understanding election modeling, public opinion tracking, and sentiment analysis using digital tools will allow them to develop deeper insights into political behavior and governance. The ability to analyze and interpret large datasets will become an essential skill for anyone seeking to understand voter behavior, predict policy outcomes, or assess international conflicts.

Political science education must also adapt to the growing influence of digital media. Universities should introduce courses on analyzing propaganda, detecting misinformation, and understanding media influence on public perception. Encouraging students to develop critical media literacy skills will help them navigate the modern information landscape, where political messaging is often manipulated for strategic purposes. Without these skills, individuals may struggle to differentiate between legitimate political discourse and deceptive narratives designed to influence public opinion.

In addition to preparing students for traditional careers in government and academia, political science programs must embrace non-traditional career pathways such as political consulting, policy entrepreneurship, ed-tech, and media analysis. The rise of digital platforms and political startups offers new opportunities for individuals to engage with political issues in innovative ways. Providing mentorship for students looking to launch startups in civic technology, election forecasting, and public policy solutions can open new doors for political science graduates. The future of the field will not be confined to bureaucratic institutions but will extend into technology firms, think tanks, and grassroots organizations that leverage digital tools for political engagement.

Preparing students for ethical and responsible leadership is equally critical. Political science education must emphasize moral reasoning, ethical dilemmas, and accountability in governance. Encouraging students to analyze historical and contemporary ethical failures in politics will help them understand the long-term impact of their decisions. Case studies on corruption, policy failures, and the abuse of power should be integrated into the curriculum to ensure that students develop a sense of ethical responsibility. Political science should not just teach how power works but also instill an awareness of the consequences of its misuse.

As we look ahead, political science education must embrace change while maintaining its core purpose: to equip individuals with the knowledge, skills, and ethical grounding to shape a more just and effective political system. The next generation of political scientists must be data-savvy, globally aware, technologically equipped, and morally grounded. By integrating modern tools, interdisciplinary knowledge, and experiential learning, educators and students alike can shape a more informed, responsible, and engaged political landscape. The challenge ahead is not just about understanding politics but about reshaping it for the better. Political science must not only analyze the world—it must equip individuals to change it.

CHAPTER THIRTEEN

Sample Lesson Plans & Case Study-Based Learning Models

Sample Lesson Plans & Case Study-Based Learning Models

Sample Lesson Plans & Case Study-Based Learning Models

To enhance political science education and bridge the gap between theoretical knowledge and real-world applications, this section presents sample lesson plans and case study-based learning models. These resources aim to make political science more interactive, engaging, and relevant for students by integrating structured discussions, problem-solving activities, and technology-driven tools.

Sample Lesson Plan: Understanding Electoral Systems Through Simulations

Objective: Students will explore different electoral systems (First-Past-the-Post, Proportional Representation, Ranked-Choice Voting) and analyze their impact on governance and representation.

Activity: The class will be divided into political parties, and a simulated election will be conducted using different voting systems. Students will analyze the outcomes and discuss the strengths and weaknesses of each system.

Assessment: Students will write a reflection on how electoral systems influence political stability, voter representation, and policy outcomes.

Sample Lesson Plan: Policy Analysis and Advocacy Workshop

Objective: To develop critical thinking skills and understand the policymaking process.

Activity: Students will be assigned a contemporary policy issue (such as climate change legislation, digital privacy laws, or social welfare programs) and will work in groups to draft a policy proposal. They will then present their proposals in a simulated policy debate.

Assessment: Evaluation based on research depth, argument clarity, and policy feasibility.

Case Study-Based Learning Models

1. Case Study: The Arab Spring and Digital Activism
Objective: To analyze how social media influenced political movements and the role of digital tools in modern democracy.

Activity: Students will examine key moments from the Arab Spring, identify the role of digital platforms like Twitter and Facebook, and discuss the ethical considerations of digital activism.

Assessment: A comparative analysis of digital activism in different global protests.

2. Case Study: Cambridge Analytica and Data Ethics in Politics
Objective: To understand how data analytics can influence voter behavior and the ethical implications of digital campaigning.

Activity: Students will explore how Cambridge Analytica used personal data to micro-target voters and debate the necessity of stronger regulations on political advertising.

Assessment: A written analysis on balancing political marketing and data privacy.

3. Case Study: The Indian General Elections and the Role of AI in Voter Mobilization
Objective: To explore how artificial intelligence and big data are reshaping political campaigning in India.

Activity: Students will investigate AI-driven campaign strategies used in recent Indian elections, including sentiment analysis, chatbot-based voter engagement, and predictive polling.

Assessment: A group presentation on AI's future in democratic governance.

These sample lesson plans and case study models aim to equip students with analytical, research, and problem-solving skills necessary for navigating complex political issues. By fostering active engagement and critical thinking, they prepare students for leadership roles in governance, policy analysis, and advocacy in an increasingly digital and interconnected world.

CHAPTER FOURTEEN

List of Digital Tools, Political Science Journals, and Research Resources

List of Digital Tools, Political Science Journals, and Research Resources

To support students, educators, and researchers in political science, this section provides a comprehensive list of digital tools, academic journals, and research resources. These resources help in conducting data-driven analysis, staying updated with the latest political science developments, and improving research methodologies.

Digital Tools for Political Science Research and Analysis

1. R and Python – Used for statistical analysis, data visualization, and political modeling.

2. Tableau and Power BI – Data visualization tools to analyze election trends, public policy, and governance data.

3. Geographic Information System (GIS) Tools (ArcGIS, QGIS) – For spatial analysis of political and electoral data.

4. Google Scholar & Semantic Scholar – Search engines for academic papers and political science literature.

5. Zotero & Mendeley – Reference management tools to organize citations and research materials.

6. Polity IV Project & V-Dem Dataset – Resources for analyzing democracy indices and governance structures worldwide.

7. LexisNexis & ProQuest – Databases for legal and political science research.

8. FactCheck.org & AltNews – Tools for verifying political claims and combating misinformation.

9. OpenSecrets & PRS India – Platforms for analyzing political funding, lobbying, and legislation.

10. ChatGPT & Claude AI – AI-driven research assistants to generate insights and summarize political literature.

Leading Political Science Journals

1. American Political Science Review (APSR) – Covers all major fields of political science, including political theory, comparative politics, and international relations.

2. World Politics – A top journal focusing on international relations and comparative politics.

3. Journal of Democracy – Explores democratic institutions, governance, and political transitions globally.

4. Public Opinion Quarterly – Focuses on public opinion, voter behavior, and polling analysis.

5. Foreign Affairs – Provides analysis on global political trends, diplomacy, and security studies.

6. The Review of International Studies – Covers international relations theories and case studies.

7. Comparative Political Studies – Examines political institutions, elections, and governance across different nations.

8. Political Science Quarterly – Publishes research on political thought, governance, and domestic/international politics.

9. The Indian Journal of Political Science – Features research on Indian and South Asian politics.

10. Global Policy Journal – Focuses on policy making, economic governance, and international relations.

Research Resources and Databases

1. UN Data & World Bank Open Data – Provides economic, social, and political data for global research.

2. The Brookings Institution & RAND Corporation – Leading think tanks producing policy research.

3. International Institute for Strategic Studies (IISS) – Research on defense and security policies.

4. European Council on Foreign Relations (ECFR) – Analysis on European and global diplomacy.

5. Election Commission of India & Lokniti-CSDS – Official election data and voter surveys in India.

6. The Hague Academy of International Law – Legal and political research resources.

7. Harvard Dataverse & ICPSR – Repositories for social science datasets and political surveys.

8. Chatham House & Carnegie Endowment for International Peace – Policy think tanks focusing on global governance.

9. The Open Government Partnership (OGP) – Research on transparency and democratic governance.

10. MIT Election Data and Science Lab – US election data and research on voting trends.

These tools, journals, and research databases empower students and professionals to conduct rigorous political science research, analyze policy trends, and contribute to scholarly debates. By integrating these resources into their studies, learners can develop a deeper understanding of global political dynamics and policy-making.

References

Books & Academic Papers

1. Acemoglu, D., & Robinson, J. A. (2012). Why nations fail: The origins of power, prosperity, and poverty. Crown Business.

2. Almond, G. A., & Verba, S. (1963). The civic culture: Political attitudes and democracy in five nations. Princeton University Press.

3. Barber, B. R. (1984). Strong democracy: Participatory politics for a new age. University of California Press.

4. Bennett, W. L., & Segerberg, A. (2013). The logic of connective action: Digital media and the personalization of contentious politics. Cambridge University Press.

5. Bimber, B. (2003). Information and American democracy: Technology in the evolution of political power. Cambridge University Press.

6. Castells, M. (2010). The rise of the network society. Wiley-Blackwell.

7. Dahl, R. A. (1989). Democracy and its critics. Yale University Press.

8. Diamond, L. (2019). Ill winds: Saving democracy from Russian rage, Chinese ambition, and American complacency. Penguin.

9. Druckman, J. N., & Lupia, A. (2016). Cambridge handbook of experimental political science. Cambridge University Press.

10. Fiorina, M. P. (2002). Culture war? The myth of a polarized America. Pearson Longman.

11. Fishkin, J. S. (2009). When the people speak: Deliberative democracy and public consultation. Oxford University Press.

12. Flinders, M. (2012). Defending politics: Why democracy matters in the twenty-first century. Oxford University Press.

13. Fukuyama, F. (2011). The origins of political order: From prehuman times to the French Revolution. Farrar, Straus and Giroux.

14. Huntington, S. P. (1996). The clash of civilizations and the remaking of world order. Simon & Schuster.

15. Iyengar, S. (2019). Media politics: A citizen's guide. W. W. Norton.

16. Kahneman, D. (2011). Thinking, fast and slow. Farrar, Straus and Giroux.

17. Kautilya. (1992). Arthashastra (L. N. Rangarajan, Trans.). Penguin Books.

18. Lakoff, G. (2004). Don't think of an elephant! Know your values and frame the debate. Chelsea Green Publishing.

19. Lijphart, A. (2012). Patterns of democracy: Government forms and performance in thirty-six countries. Yale University Press.

20. Levitsky, S., & Ziblatt, D. (2018). How democracies die. Crown Publishing.

Journals & Research Articles

21. Aldrich, J. H. (1995). Why parties? The origin and transformation of political parties in America. American Political Science Review, 89(3), 712-728.

22. Bartels, L. M. (2008). Economic inequality and political representation. Perspectives on Politics, 6(1), 15-31.

23. Baum, M. A., & Groeling, T. (2008). New media and the polarization of American political discourse. Political Communication, 25(4), 345-365.

24. Bennett, W. L. (2012). The personalization of politics: Political identity, social media, and changing patterns of participation. Annals of the American Academy of Political and Social Science, 644(1), 20-39.

25. Bimber, B. (2014). Digital media in the Obama campaigns of 2008 and 2012. The International Journal of Press/Politics, 19(4), 436-457.

26. Chauchard, S. (2018). Can democracy survive disinformation? Journal of Democracy, 29(2), 56-68.

27. Faris, R., & Benkler, Y. (2018). A field guide to media manipulation. Harvard Law Review, 131(2), 568-612.

28. Flynn, D. J., Nyhan, B., & Reifler, J. (2017). The nature and origins of misperceptions: Understanding false and unsupported beliefs about politics. Political Psychology, 38(S1), 127-150.

29. Green, D. P., & Gerber, A. S. (2015). Get out the vote: How to increase voter turnout. Annual Review of Political Science, 18, 101-119.

30. Guess, A. M., Nyhan, B., & Reifler, J. (2020). Exposure to untrustworthy websites in the 2016 US election. Nature Human Behaviour, 4(5), 472-480.

Government Reports & Think Tank Publications

31. Brookings Institution. (2020). AI and the future of democracy. Brookings Press.

32. Carnegie Endowment for International Peace. (2018). Cyber warfare and national security.

33. Center for Strategic and International Studies. (2019). The impact of social media on political polarization.

34. Chatham House. (2021). Blockchain and digital governance.

35. European Council on Foreign Relations. (2017). The rise of cyber diplomacy.

36. Pew Research Center. (2018). Social media, political engagement, and public opinion trends.

37. RAND Corporation. (2020). How artificial intelligence is transforming political campaigns.

38. The Hague Academy of International Law. (2019). Digital democracy: Prospects and challenges.

39. Transparency International. (2020). Fighting political corruption in the digital age.

40. UNDP. (2021). AI and digital governance: Ethics, regulation, and democracy.

Case Studies & Reports on Elections and Digital Politics

41. BBC. (2018). The role of social media in the Cambridge Analytica scandal.

42. The Guardian. (2019). How misinformation shaped the Brexit referendum.

43. The New York Times. (2020). The 2016 US elections and Russian cyber influence.

44. The Hindu. (2021). Fake news, elections, and democracy in India.

45. The Wire. (2019). India's election commission and digital voting concerns.

46. MIT Election Data and Science Lab. (2021). Big data and voter behavior analysis.

47. Open Government Partnership. (2020). E-governance and transparency in policymaking.

48. PRS India. (2018). Legislative research in India: Challenges and progress.

49. World Economic Forum. (2019). The future of AI-driven political campaigns.

50. Reuters Institute. (2020). Trust in digital news and political misinformation.